THE JOB HUNTER'S FINAL EXAM

(with all the answers!)

by
THOMAS M. CAMDEN

SURREY BOOKS
101 East Erie Street
Suite 900
Chicago, Illinois 60611-2811

The Job Hunter's Final Exam is published by Surrey Books, 101 E. Erie Street, Suite 900, Chicago, IL 60611. Telephone: (312) 751-7330.

This book is manufactured in the United States of America.

2nd Edition, completely revised and re-set. 1 2 3 4 5

Library of Congress Cataloging-in-Publication data:

Camden, Thomas M., 1938-
    The job hunter's final exam/by Thomas M. Camden.—2nd ed.
    156 p.   cm.

ISBN 0-940625-21-0
    1. Job hunting—Problems, exercises, etc. I. Title.
    HF5382.7.C36 1990   89-27480
    650.14'076—dc20   CIP

Single copies may be ordered directly from Surrey Books at the address above. Send check or money order for $10.95 per book (which includes postage and handling). For quantity discounts, please contact the publisher.

Editorial production by Bookcrafters, Inc.

Cover design by Hughes Design

Typesetting by On Track

This book is dedicated to my children Bernadette, Matthew, Catherine, Paul, and Dominic...and their children. May your work always be an important part of your life, but never the purpose of it.

ACKNOWLEDGMENTS

The author wishes to thank the following people for their help: Publisher Susan Schwartz; Production Editor Gene DeRoin; Editorial Consultant Valjean McLenighan; Art Director Sally Hughes.

CONTENTS

FOREWORD
How To Use This Book

When I lost a job for the first time, years ago, the advice that was available in written form was so theoretical that it had little value to me. The advice books on the market today, however, are really quite good. The problem is that few people read them from cover to cover. Those who do seldom understand or apply the principles taught.

Thus, the reason for this unique approach: *The Job Hunter's Final Exam.* By taking the test, scoring yourself, studying the answers, and taking the test again, you should automatically learn the principles and techniques I've developed in some 30 years as a personnel professional and human resources consultant. Over the years, I've worked with thousands of job hunters, which qualifies me as an expert—if not through trial and error alone, then through the successes and learning I shared with men and women of every background and salary level.

So take my advice: read this book from cover to cover. It should be easy for you, and I hope it will help you to obtain the right job sooner, with less pain and fewer mistakes than you might otherwise make. Take the test first, score yourself, read the answers, and take the test again. You'll be amazed at how well-informed you've become.

Good luck—and happy hunting.

Thomas M. Camden

THE QUIZ
How Much Do You Really Know?

1. Take the test.
2. Score yourself.
3. Read the answers.
4. Take the test again (it's repeated in the back of the book).
5. Score yourself again, and see how much you've progressed.

1 Most people are able to find a job in a week or two. If it takes longer than a month, something is terribly wrong.

☐ **TRUE** ✓☐ **FALSE**

2 The first paragraph of your resume should contain a thorough explanation of your employment objective.

☐ **TRUE** ✓☐ **FALSE**

3 The federal, state, and local governments are still excellent employers.

☐ **TRUE** ✓☐ **FALSE**

4 During an economic recession, recent graduates have a better chance for jobs if they have an MBA.

☐ **TRUE** ✓☐ **FALSE**

5 Being unemployed is an embarrassment, so if you lost your last job, it's best to keep it to yourself.

☐ **TRUE** ✓☐ **FALSE**

6 It's better to be unemployed than underemployed.

☐ **TRUE** ✓☐ **FALSE**

7 Someone who loses a job or gets fired should take a few weeks off before starting a search in order to sort things out.

☐ **TRUE** ✓☐ **FALSE**

8 Maintaining a positive outlook about job hunting has very little value if the national unemployment rate exceeds 9 percent or the local rate exceeds 14 percent.

☐ **TRUE** ✓☐ **FALSE**

9 There is no such thing as a perfectly secure job.

✓☐ **TRUE** ☐ **FALSE**

10 Companies don't hire people. People hire people.

✓☐ **TRUE** ☐ **FALSE**

11 The first step in any job search is to develop an outstanding resume.

☐ **TRUE**　　✓☐ **FALSE**

12 The length of any resume should be:

A ☐ One page

B ☐ Two pages

C ☐ Three pages

✓ **D** ☐ As long as needed

13 If the job hunter is particularly attractive, it's a good idea to include a picture with the resume.

☐ **TRUE**　　✓☐ **FALSE**

14 Any time a job hunter answers an advertisement, a cover letter must accompany the resume.

✓ ☐ **TRUE**　　☐ **FALSE**

15 It's important to include every job you ever held when writing a resume.

☐ **TRUE**　　✓☐ **FALSE**

16 When a company asks you to complete an employment application form, an effective resume will suffice.

☐ **TRUE**　　✓☐ **FALSE**

17 Always list your salary on your resume.

☐ **TRUE**　　✓☐ **FALSE**

18 Always list references on your resume.

☐ TRUE   ✓☐ FALSE

19 If you have just a couple of college courses and no degree, it's O.K. to state in your resume that you completed "two years" at a college or university.

☐ TRUE   ✓☐ FALSE

20 It's a good idea to include height and weight in the personal section of the resume, particularly if the job hunter is tall.

☐ TRUE   ✓☐ FALSE

21 It's important to include your social security number on the resume to prove you've registered.

☐ TRUE   ☐ FALSE

22 If the job hunter doesn't have a typewriter, it's acceptable to write the cover letter in longhand, provided it's on personal stationery.

☐ TRUE   ☐ FALSE

23 Hiring a professional writer to prepare a resume is the way to make the best impression.

☐ TRUE   ☐ FALSE

24 The resume is a sales tool, so the more self-praise and accomplishments it contains, the better it will be.

☐ TRUE   ☐ FALSE

25 Your reason for leaving each previous job must be stated in the resume.

☐ TRUE ✓☐ FALSE

26 "Networking" means talking to important people who have jobs.

☐ TRUE ✓☐ FALSE

27 In networking, a wide array of people who provide services can become excellent sources of job leads.

☐ TRUE ✓☐ FALSE

28 Companies that visit college placement offices to recruit seldom hire "C" students.

☐ TRUE ✓☐ FALSE

29 The job search process requires about 20 hours of effort each week.

☐ TRUE ✓☐ FALSE

30 Professional directories are excellent sources of information for every job hunter.

✓☐ TRUE ☐ FALSE

31 Any fraternity or alumni list has value to the job hunter, providing the hunter has been out of school less than four years.

✓☐ TRUE ☐ FALSE

32 The personnel department does all the hiring and firing, so that's the first place to contact to get an interview.

☐ TRUE ✓☐ FALSE

33 Most employers are inundated with unsolicited resumes. It makes sense to be a bit assertive and show up in person to request an interview rather than to send paper.

☐ TRUE ✓☐ FALSE

34 The easiest part of the job search is the interview.

✓☐ TRUE ☐ FALSE

35 Sending 100 resumes to 100 different company presidents is certain to generate at least 10 interviews.

☐ TRUE ✓☐ FALSE

36 The old adage, "See someone who knows someone," is the heart of networking, the best technique for getting interviews.

✓☐ TRUE ☐ FALSE

37 A guaranteed way to generate employment interviews is to run an advertisement describing skills, experience, and salary.

☐ TRUE ✓☐ FALSE

38 Employment agencies can get you a good job.

☐ TRUE ✓☐ FALSE

39 A school's placement office can assist in the search if the job hunter is a graduate of that school.

✓☐ TRUE ☐ FALSE

40 Employment agencies work on a contingency basis, so they really do not benefit the job hunter.

✓ ☐ **TRUE**   ☐ **FALSE**

41 "Headhunter" refers to employment agencies, executive search firms, and career counselors.

☐ **TRUE**   ✓ ☐ **FALSE**

42 Employment agency contracts are all identical since they are state-regulated.

☐ **TRUE**   ✓ ☐ **FALSE**

43 Answering help-wanted ads is an integral part of any job search but is usually not too productive.

✓ ☐ **TRUE**   ☐ **FALSE**

44 In answering an ad, it's best not to include a salary requirement or present salary even if the ad requests salary data.

✓ ☐ **TRUE**   ☐ **FALSE**

45 Companies that run blind advertisements (do not reveal their identity) do so because they don't want their employees to know they are advertising.

✓ ☐ **TRUE**   ☐ **FALSE**

46 Military experience is an important part of a person's life and should be thoroughly discussed in an employment interview.

☐ **TRUE**   ✓ ☐ **FALSE**

47 Which of the following questions is illegal and cannot be asked by a prospective employer?

    A ☐ Have you ever been convicted of a crime?

    B ☐ Why were you fired from your last job?

    C ☐ Are you currently receiving unemployment compensation?

    ✓ **D** ☐ What was your father's occupation?

48 An employment interview is a sales presentation by the applicant, so the job hunter must sell experience, personality, potential, and strengths.

    ✓☐ **TRUE**   ☐ **FALSE**

49 "Are you open to relocation?" is a common interview question. If the job hunter doesn't want to move, the best answer is "No!"

    ✓☐ **TRUE**   ☐ **FALSE**

50 When asked the very common question, "What are your strengths and weaknesses?" it's a good idea to be modest about strengths and perfectly honest about limitations.

    ☐ **TRUE**   ✓☐ **FALSE**

51 When an interviewer asks what you do in your spare time, he or she really wants to know if you have bad habits.

□ TRUE   □ FALSE

52 When the subject of salary comes up during the interview the job seeker should automatically ask for a salary 15 percent higher than the present or last salary.

□ TRUE   □ FALSE

53 If a job seeker talks about background, grade school and high school activities should never be mentioned.

□ TRUE   □ FALSE

54 Ten or 15 years after college, your grade point average is of no interest to the interviewer.

□ TRUE   □ FALSE

55 The decision to hire or not to hire is generally made in the first five minutes of the interview.

□ TRUE   □ FALSE

56 An interviewer has a right to ask an applicant's net worth.

□ TRUE   □ FALSE

57 If an interviewer is rude or a "jerk," the best tactic is to get up and leave rather than continue.

□ TRUE   □ FALSE

58 When asked to describe your strengths, it's good to use words such as "aggressive," "assertive," and "ambitious."

    □ TRUE   √□ FALSE

59 If asked, "Tell me about your spouse," the best answer is to advise the interviewer politely that the question is illegal.

    √□ TRUE   □ FALSE

60 It's ill advised to ask an applicant, "What branch of the military did you serve in?"

    □ TRUE   √□ FALSE

61 "How's your health?" is an illegal question.

    □ TRUE   √□ FALSE

62 It's best to show up for an interview at least 20 to 30 minutes early.

    □ TRUE   √□ FALSE

63 To prepare for employment interviews, companies always thoroughly read the applicant's resume and sometimes make reference checks before the interview.

    □ TRUE   √□ FALSE

64 College honors, self-supported tuition, fraternity or sorority offices held, and the like have little place in the interview.

    □ TRUE   √□ FALSE

65 To ease tension and establish rapport with the interviewer in the first five minutes, it's a good idea to tell a joke or two.

☐ **TRUE** ✓☐ **FALSE**

66 Smoking or chewing gum during an interview may cause the interviewer to reject an applicant.

✓☐ **TRUE** ☐ **FALSE**

67 Common sense dictates that people should dress conservatively for an interview, avoiding gaudy clothing or extreme styles.

✓☐ **TRUE** ☐ **FALSE**

68 A winning smile and a firm handshake can make the difference between "winning" or "losing" in an interview.

✓☐ **TRUE** ☐ **FALSE**

69 Before the employment interview, the applicant should do some homework on the company. It's poor form to ask the interviewer, "What does your company do?"

✓☐ **TRUE** ☐ **FALSE**

70 A supply of resumes, a contact list, a calendar, and a job log are the briefcase contents every job seeker should carry to every interview.

✓☐ **TRUE** ☐ **FALSE**

71 What a person says in the interview determines whether he or she gets the offer.

☐ TRUE   ✓☐ FALSE

72 When the interviewer says, "Tell me about yourself," the interviewer really wants to know only about your personality.

✓☐ TRUE   ☐ FALSE

73 If there are a few applicants for one position, the person with the best technical qualifications generally gets the offer.

✓☐ TRUE   ☐ FALSE

74 Most employers are willing to spend time with anyone interested in getting a job in their company.

☐ TRUE   ✓☐ FALSE

75 Anytime the national unemployment rate exceeds 9 percent, it's almost impossible to get a job.

✓☐ TRUE   ☐ FALSE

76 Pre-employment polygraph (lie-detector) tests are against the law.

☐ TRUE   ✓☐ FALSE

77 It's best to look for another job while you are still employed.

✓☐ TRUE   ☐ FALSE

78 If a job hunter wants to work in another city, it's best to move there first and then start looking.

☐ TRUE ☐ FALSE

79 Most employment managers consider it a breach of ethics for an employee to look for another job on company time.

☐ TRUE ☐ FALSE

80 During the interview, it's best to avoid any personal information about family background, marriage, children, or the like.

☐ TRUE ☐ FALSE

81 It is illegal for an employer to ask an applicant about marital status or religious background.

☐ TRUE ☐ FALSE

82 If a job hunter is divorced, an employer can ask who has custody of the children.

☐ TRUE ☐ FALSE

83 Most personnel people regard divorce as a sign of failure, so never volunteer that information in a resume or interview.

☐ TRUE ☐ FALSE

84 Always include the statement, "In excellent health," in the personal section of your resume no matter what your health condition is.

☐ TRUE ☐ FALSE

85 Beards and long hair on men are still perceived negatively, even if the beard is handsomely trimmed.

☑ ☐ **TRUE**   ☐ **FALSE**

86 Anyone with graying hair who is looking for a new job had best color or dye it to look younger.

☐ **TRUE**   ☑ ☐ **FALSE**

87 People over 50, women, blacks, and the unemployed are generally discriminated against in the employment process.

☑ ☐ **TRUE**   ☐ **FALSE**

88 Most people in the work force are college graduates.

☐ **TRUE**   ☑ ☐ **FALSE**

89 Reference checks are still an important element of the job search; references should be carefully prepared.

☑ ☐ **TRUE**   ☐ **FALSE**

90 Employers really don't have the time to verify previous employment or educational background and seldom do so.

☐ **TRUE**   ☑ ☐ **FALSE**

91 If your references include important people—authors, judges, sports figures—it's a good idea to include them on your resume to make it more impressive.

☐ **TRUE**   ☑ ☐ **FALSE**

92 Personnel departments cannot legally verify salaries of former employees, so the job hunter can claim any salary he/she likes.

☐ TRUE   ✓☐ FALSE

93 Formal employment contracts are usually provided only to senior executives.

✓☐ TRUE   ☐ FALSE

94 An employer extending a job offer expects to wait at least three weeks for an answer.

☐ TRUE   ✓☐ FALSE

95 A formal offer of employment is a letter outlining title, salary, reporting relationships, benefits, and other important aspects of the job. Without such a letter, there is no formal offer.

✓☐ TRUE   ☐ FALSE

96 Temporary work often leads to permanent employment, so it makes sense to accept a temporary job as soon as possible.

☐ TRUE   ✓☐ FALSE

97 Getting a good score on a civil service test guarantees a job offer.

☐ TRUE   ✓☐ FALSE

98 A company can fire an employee who lied about anything on the employment application form.

✓☐ TRUE   ☐ FALSE

99 Sometimes the hiring authority in a department, if sufficiently impressed by the candidate, can create a new job.

√☐ **TRUE**   ☐ **FALSE**

100 "Overqualified" is a rejection excuse that really means "too old."

√☐ **TRUE**   ☐ **FALSE**

YOUR SCORE

Number of Correct Answers	Comments
Less Than 50	Big Trouble! Don't start your job search until you study the answers and try again.
50-59	At least you got half the answers correct. Of course, you could have done as well flipping a coin. Study the answers and try again.
60-69	Below average, but that's O.K. This book can help you improve your job-hunting skills.
70-79	Average. Who wants to be average? Study the answers to become superb.
80-89	Above average—but you can possibly improve on the next try.

90-95   Excellent—two standard
deviations above the mean.

96-99   Superb—you are now ready to
succeed in a job search.

100   Impossible. Nobody gets 100!

ANSWERS 1-10
Objectives—How To Begin

Successful job hunters complete a number of important steps before landing job offers. They write a resume, send cover letters, and schedule interviews, to name a few. These steps become secondary, however, for most students about to enter the "real" job market for the first time. The job *objective* should really be their most important consideration.

A job objective, or strategy, is really a goal. It helps answer the question, "What kind of job or jobs should I consider, based on who I am, what I've done, what I want to do, what I can do, and what I should do?"

Unfortunately, this is a difficult question, especially at this point in time. Many people still don't have an answer at age 43 or 53. Why? Because they fail to do the homework and personal assessment necessary to establish a job-search target or objective.

Dozens of questions must be answered before setting up your first job interview. The answers will help form the foundation of your strategy. Then you need to examine what aspects of a job will really give you professional satisfaction.

A recent graduate often feels, "With my debts, satisfaction means money!" That's a normal response, but there's more to consider. You also have to think about what you are prepared to do to get the money you want. Would you break the law? Compromise your integrity? Purposely hurt people? Provide products or services you don't respect? Work with people you can't tolerate? Work 60-hour weeks, nights, and weekends? Probably not. Although there are people who are motivated solely by money, most of us have a more balanced outlook. Money is important, but so are the other aspects of the job.

Let's say you have good interpersonal skills and, therefore, want a job that involves people. Your training may be in marketing or sales. You like to travel and don't want to be stuck behind a desk for life. The ability to grow in a job also is important to you. Based on these facts, it's clear that salary is only one of many job variables you must consider.

Before you go charging into your first employment interview, take time to decide what you want to accomplish. The following questions are designed to assist you in determining your standard of values, ambitions, life goals, and productivity. You'll probably find it useful to write down your answers.

Describe yourself.

Describe the kind of person others think you are.

What do you want to accomplish with your life?

What role does your job play in that goal?

What impact do you have on other people?

What are your accomplishments to date?

What still needs to be accomplished?

What were your extracurricular activities in school?

Did you exert a leadership role in any of these activities?

Is your career part of your life or all of it?

In past jobs, what did you enjoy most? Least?

What job would perfectly match your talents and interests?

What responsibilities do you want to avoid?

How hard do you really want to work?

What kind of manager are you?

How self-disciplined are you?

What kind of subordinate and team player are you?

How can your job make you happier?

If you were ever fired from a job, what were the reasons?

What are the 10 most important things you're looking for in a job?

Your answers also will help you understand your preferences and strengths as well as the abilities and experience you want to market. This personal assessment also should reveal certain "negatives" about yourself, that is, your limitations or responsibilities you don't want to assume. If you can't manage people or don't want to, for heaven's sake, don't seek a job as a manager; it won't work.

If you are honest and thorough in your self-evaluation, it will become clear which job elements are important to you. You'll avoid the mistake of seeking a job for which you are underqualified or overqualified.

Accomplishing any objective depends on knowledge, ability, and dozens of other variables. Before continuing, ask yourself if your objective really is attainable. This does not mean that you should abandon your dreams. An objective may only seem unrealistic and unattainable now because of lack of experience or other factors. We all need dreams and hopes to help activate our potential and encourage us to set high goals. But it's important to keep dreams in proper perspective.

You must be able to distinguish between practical, attainable goals and fantasy. Ask yourself, "What kind of job or jobs should I be looking for, and why?" This will help you get a handle on the kind of job you need and the kind an employer can realistically offer.

The questions you answered here will prepare you for employment interviews since employers often ask many of the same questions. Here are some additional questions you may be asked:

> What kind of job are you looking for?
> What are your short-term goals?
> What are your long-term goals?
> Why do you want to work for us?
> Why should I hire you?

Once you understand what you realistically want, you can focus on finding the appropriate jobs and employers. And with an objective in mind, you'll know which direction to take.

Do you remember that great passage from Lewis Carroll's *Alice in Wonderland?* Alice was lost, so she asked the Cheshire Cat, "Would you tell me, please, which way I ought to go from here?"

"That depends a good deal on where you want to get to," said the Cat.

"I don't much care where," said Alice.

"Then it doesn't matter which way you walk."

Unless you want to be like Alice—not much caring where you get to—the first step in your job search will be to establish an objective.

---

1   *Most people are able to find a job in a week or two. If it takes longer than a month, something is terribly wrong.*

FALSE. A thorough search of the job market and review of alternatives requires much more time than a week or two. Some career experts use formulas to estimate the average length of a job search. One counselor suggests that it takes two weeks of looking for every $6,000 earned yearly. Another figures one month of looking for every $10,000 in annual earnings. Perhaps it's best to ignore the averages and just be prepared to invest two or three months, if possible.

Certain jobs are almost always available because of high turnover. Among these are straight commission sales, retail clerking, waiting tables, fast food counter work, driving jobs, etc. People who accept such positions after looking for only a week or two are often under self-imposed pressure to get back to work as soon as possible. They may be embarrassed about being unemployed and assume falsely that their search for a permanent position can continue just as effectively while they are employed in a stop-gap job.

If at all possible, take the time required to review the market carefully. The first opportunity seldom is the best. If there is a doubt, keep looking as long as your resources permit.

2 *The first paragraph of your resume should contain a thorough explanation of your employment objective.*

FALSE. If the job hunter lists a very specific objective in the resume, he or she is seldom considered for other opportunities. A job search is an effort to investigate all available opportunities and to discover jobs that may not have been considered initially. If a microbiologist's objective is to teach microbiology, he probably eliminated himself from consideration for work in industry, consulting, or the government.

On the other hand, many objectives are so broad that they really mean very little. For example:

> OBJECTIVE: Senior-level management position in public relations, employee communication, or marketing communications with a major company.

Broad objectives turn off the reader. Some job hunters print up six different resumes with a half-dozen different objectives. That really isn't necessary. One resume is enough. Unless your objective is so precise that you will consider no alternatives, my recommendation is to omit the objective from the resume and include it in the cover letter.

---

3 *The federal, state, and local governments are still excellent employers.*

TRUE. The Bureau of Labor Statistics confirms that service industries employ more people than those providing goods. No one provides more services than our governments! And the demand is increasing, particularly for health and welfare, police and fire protection. Despite the current emphasis on limiting government growth, government employees make up about 16 percent of the working population. This means that more than nine million people are on the public payroll.

A few examples:

> In the 1980s, 48,000 people worked as government construction inspectors at an average salary of $19,500.

> More than 275,000 fire fighters enjoyed salaries ranging from $13,000 to $20,500.

> There were 495,000 full-time police officers in local police and sheriff's departments who were paid an average of $15,200 yearly. Many salaries exceeded $20,000. The 55,000 state police averaged $14,000 yearly with a top salary of $23,800.

> The Post Office employed 250,000 mail carriers in 1980 at an average salary of $19,275. The 265,000 postal clerks earned an average of $19,222 a year. Part-time people earn $9.05 per hour and advance to $10.38 after eight years.

In short, government pay is the highest it has ever been; benefits include extensive vacations and numerous holidays.

---

4 *During an economic recession, recent graduates have a better chance for jobs if they have an MBA.*

FALSE. However, there are arguments for both sides. Having a graduate degree is, in the abstract, better than not having one. But in a recessionary economy most employers want to increase revenue and reduce expenses, starting with the biggest expense, the payroll. And an employee with an MBA usually costs more than one without.

Of course, if the MBA graduate will work for the same salary as a non-MBA, the MBA will have an edge. The employer, however, may expect that a low-paid MBA will soon leave for a better offer.

MBA or not, employers must also consider the expense of training a recent graduate. During an economic downturn, training and recruiting programs are usually the first to go. Then come hiring freezes. (Sometimes older employees are replaced with younger, less expensive employees; such practices, however, are against the law.)

Recent undergraduates who have difficulty landing their first job may think that going back for an MBA will increase their marketability. Not necessarily; the money invested in graduate education may eventually bear fruit, but perhaps not for five years or more. Meanwhile, the student has lost two years of possible full-time, marketable experience. The young undergraduate who works for those two years is that much ahead of the game.

Many employers now prefer their employees to obtain graduate degrees on a part-time basis while accruing full-time practical experience. Of course it takes much longer, but from the employer's point of view, the graduate courses selected are usually more applicable. From the student's point of view, part-time graduate work can be a way to have tuition and books underwritten, at least in part, by the employer.

5   Being unemployed is an embarrassment, so if you lost your last job, it's best to keep it to yourself.

FALSE. There is a stigma attached to being unemployed in this country, but most of the guilt and embarrassment is self-imposed. We tend to think that others will say, "If she's out of work, she probably deserves it!"

Foreign competition, plant closings, a recession, acquisitions, mergers, divestitures, cutbacks, and dozens of other reasons for job loss have not eliminated the trauma of being terminated. But "keeping it to yourself" will not lessen the pain as much as it will prolong the unemployment. Networking is the best technique I know of for generating interviews—and networking requires you to tell people you know that you're looking for a job. Networking doesn't mean going around "hat in hand," asking for work. It means recruiting personal resources to assist in marketing yourself.

6   It's better to be unemployed than underemployed.

TRUE. Underemployment means being in a position that requires less ability than you have. Underemployed workers are, unavoidably, dissatisfied and wish to change jobs. Eventually their performance is affected and their attitude begins to influence fellow workers. If the situation continues, the underemployed worker is eventually fired.

Underemployed job hunters not only are unhappy in their jobs, but are restricted in their search for better alternatives. Unemployed, they would have the time to find a job that uses their full abilities.

---

7 *Someone who loses a job or gets fired should take a few weeks off before starting a search in order to sort things out.*

FALSE. Most people feel "let down" immediately following the loss of a job; the normal desire is to go into seclusion before beginning the awesome task of a job search. It becomes even more tempting when a generous severance arrangement, cashed-in profit sharing, or unused vacation pay is available to relieve anxiety about money. But it is a serious mistake to take any time off. People who do so seldom rest or enjoy the time because they're really procrastinating—delaying the inevitable.

The best advice is to begin the search process immediately. Develop an objective and then set about achieving it. Take some vacation after the new job is obtained but before reporting to work. You'll enjoy yourself a lot more.

8 *Maintaining a positive outlook about job hunting has very little value if the national unemployment rate exceeds 9 percent or the local rate exceeds 14 percent.*

FALSE. Without a positive outlook, the job hunter is dead in the water. Enthusiasm, optimism, and hope must be real to face the rejection that is part of any job search. Like the little boy at the door who asks, "You don't want to buy a magazine, do you?" the job hunter who thinks that he can't succeed because of the unemployment rate is really talking himself out of a sale. With proper preparation for your search, you certainly are not permanently unemployable. With a poor attitude, however, you could be.

9 *There is no such thing as a perfectly secure job.*

TRUE. Any company for which you go to work can go out of business or be bought by another company. The person who hires you can retire, be fired or promoted, or move on to another firm. You can deliver a masterful job performance and still lose your position through no fault of your own. All this is not meant to depress or discourage you but rather to suggest that it's wiser to build security by developing your talents, marketable skills, and a solid record of achievement rather than by placing all your faith in job seniority or the stability of any single company. Keep an eye on the job market no matter how secure you may feel in your current position. Stay in touch with developments in your field, and work diligently at developing

your repertory of skills. Real security lies in confi-
dently keeping your options open.

---

10 *Companies don't hire people. People hire people.*

TRUE. One of the most significant points in this
book is that the decision to hire is made by a warm-
blooded, intelligent person who wants to do the
right thing for the company. He or she won't really
know if the decision was wise until the new employee can prove it by performance over a three-to-
six-month period. Your task is to convince the hiring authority in a one-on-one interview that you
are the best applicant.

ANSWERS 11-25
The Resume

Volumes have been written about how to write a resume. That's because, in my opinion, generations of job seekers have attached great importance to the creation and perfection of their resumes. Keep in mind that no one ever secured a job offer on the basis of a resume alone. The way to land the offer is to succeed in the employment interview. You have to convince a potential employer that you're the best person for the job. No piece of paper will do that for you.

The resume also goes by the name of curriculum vita (the course of one's life), or vita (life) for short. These terms are a little misleading, however. A resume cannot possibly tell the story of your life, especially since, as a rule, it shouldn't be more than two pages long. The French word *résumé* means "a summing up." In the American job market, a resume is a concise, written summary of your work experience, education, accomplishments, and personal background—the essentials an employer needs to evaluate your qualifications.

A resume is nothing more or less than a simple marketing tool, a printed ad for yourself. It is sometimes useful in generating interviews. But it is most effective when kept in reserve until after you've met an employer in person. Sending a follow-up letter after the interview, along with your resume, reminds the interviewer of that wonderful person he or she met last Thursday.

The Basics of a Good Resume

The resume is nothing for you to agonize over. But since almost every employer will ask you for one at some point in the hiring process, make sure that yours is a good one.

What do we mean by a good resume? First, be sure it's up to date and comprehensive. At a minimum it should include your name, address, and phone number; a complete summary of your work experience; and an education profile. (College grads need not include their high school backgrounds.)

In general, your work experience should include the name, location, and dates of employment of every job you've held since leaving school, plus a summary of your responsibilities and, most important, your accomplishments on each job. If you're a recent graduate, or have held several jobs, you can present your experience chronologically. Begin with your present position and work backward to your first job. If you haven't had that many jobs, organize your resume to emphasize the skills you've acquired through experience.

A second rule of resume-writing is to keep the resume concise. Most employers don't want to read more than two pages, and one page is preferable. In most cases your resume will be scanned, not read in detail. Describe your experience in short, pithy phrases. Avoid large blocks of copy. Your resume should read more like a chart than a short story.

There are no hard and fast rules on what to include in your resume besides work experience and education. A statement of your objective and a personal section containing date of birth, marital status, and so on, are optional. If you really are open to considering several job options, omit the objective on the resume. Leave it off completely. That will enable you to list one or two options in your cover letter that will be more targeted to your choices. In the interview you will then have the option of one, two, or even three directions rather than just the single direction stated on the resume. An employer wants to know these things about you, but it's up to you whether to include them in your resume or bring them up during the interview. If you have served in the military, you ought to mention that in your resume. All experience is beneficial, even the menial jobs.

Your salary history and references, however, should not be included in your resume; these should be discussed in person during the interview.

Keep in mind that a resume is a sales tool. Make sure that it illustrates your unique strengths in a style and format with which you can be comfortable. Indicate any unusual responsibilities you've been given or examples of how you've saved the company money or helped it grow. Include any special recognition of your ability. For example, if your salary increased substantially within a year or two, you might state the increase in terms of a percentage.

Third, keep your resume honest. Never lie, exaggerate, embellish, or deceive. Tell the truth about your education, accomplishments, and work history. You needn't account for every single work day that elapsed between jobs, however. If you left one position on June 15 and began the next on August 1, you can minimize the gap by simply listing years worked instead of months.

Fourth, your resume should have a professional look. If you type it yourself or have it typed professionally, use a high-quality office typewriter with a plastic ribbon (sometimes called a "carbon" ribbon). Do not use a household or office typewriter with a cloth ribbon.

If your budget permits, consider having your resume typeset professionally or typed on a good quality word processor. In either case you have a choice of type faces, such as boldface, italics, and small caps. You can also request that the margins be justified (lined up evenly on the right and left sides like the margins of a book).

No matter what method you use to prepare your resume, be sure to proofread it before sending it to the printer. A misspelled word or typing error reflects badly on you, even if it's not your fault. Read every word out loud, letter for letter and comma for comma.

Get a friend to help you.

Do not make copies of your resume on a photocopy machine. Have it printed professionally. The resume you leave behind after an interview or send ahead to obtain an interview may be photocopied several times by the prospective employer, and copies of copies can be very hard to read. You should also avoid such gimmicks as colored paper (unless it's very light cream or light gray) or using a paper size other than 8 1/2" x 11". Remember, the resume doesn't generate an offer, the interview does. Us the resume as a summary after the interview, whenever possible. That eliminates pre-interview judgments and allows the "screener" to respond in a positive manner following your presentation.

Now let's look at some additional points while answering the resume-related questions.

---

11 *The first step in any job search is to develop an outstanding resume.*

FALSE. The first step in a search is to develop a strategy, or an objective. Simply stated, an objective enables a person to answer the most important question: "What kind of job or jobs should I consider or do I want?"

To arrive at the answer or at least approach a conclusion, one must do a tremendous amount of introspection—reviewing past experience, personality, life objectives, value, personal needs, needs of others, expectations, dreams, goals, etc.

This exercise is to determine clearly who you are, what you want, what your gifts are, and what you have to offer. It also enables you to understand what you don't want or can't do.

Your experience is important and marketable, no matter how many jobs you've held in the past. How many times have you heard someone moan, "How can I get a job? I'm just a housewife (or student, or retiree)!"? Friends can assist in evaluating your personality, experience, and potential. Professional vocational analysis is also available.

Establishing an objective is important: it enables you to choose from available alternatives rather than merely react. But at the beginning of a job search, one seldom has an objective perfectly outlined. Many variables are unknown. The job hunter continually adds, subtracts, and fine tunes the objective as interviewing continues and more information, advice, and awareness of what the market offers are developed.

12 *The length of any resume should be:*

A ☐ *One page*
B ☐ *Two pages*
C ☐ *Three pages*
D ☐ *As long as needed*

D ☐ is the correct answer—as long as needed. Certain young people and recent graduates do not have sufficient experience to fill more than a one-page resume. Although most experts swear a resume longer than two pages will not be read, some resumes must be longer to present experience, accomplishments, and historical data effectively. A research physicist with 30 years' experience, for example, will have a difficult time meeting the two-page requirement without diluting important information and lessening the resume's effectiveness.

How you use your resume is more important than what's in it. The resume is more useful as a sales tool that *supplements* the interview than as a tool for *generating* interviews. You can send a resume in response to a help-wanted ad but so will 300 or 400 other applicants. If the ad is "open" and the company identifies itself, use every tactic you can think of to contact the hiring authority directly for an appointment rather than sending a resume to the personnel department. Leave your resume with the hiring authority after the interview to remind the hiring authority of that wonderful person he met last Thursday.

13 *If the job hunter is particularly attractive, it's a good idea to include a picture with the resume.*

FALSE. There is an unwritten rule that photographs should not accompany resumes except for actors, actresses, and models.

Photos are considered a gimmick. Personnel people get very nervous when they receive pictures, possibly because the Equal Employment Opportunity Commission has ruled that a photograph may invite discriminatory hiring practices. Don't include a picture with your resume.

14 *Any time a job hunter answers an advertisement, a cover letter must accompany the resume.*

TRUE. A help-wanted advertisement may receive hundreds of responses. The cover letter is an opportunity to supplement the resume as a sales tool. The absence of a cover letter reflects a lack of professionalism.

A cover letter should refer to the specific advertisement being answered. If the ad requests salary information, that data should be included. The cover letter should also contain additional sales points that may not be included in the resume.
For example:

> "My resume reflects 15 years' experience in office equipment sales. My specialty is selling word processing equipment, which matches your current need."

"Sales training has been part of my responsibility for the last five years, since I was promoted to area sales manager."

"My experience in building a Midwestern sales staff from scratch would be perfect for the growth plans described in your company's ad."

If possible, the cover letter should be on personal stationery of bond quality that matches the 8 1/2" x 11" resume. Stick to white or ivory. In some fields light gray is also acceptable.

---

15 It's important to include every job you ever held when writing a resume.

FALSE. Part-time jobs, summer jobs, or jobs that were short-lived do not have to be included on the resume unless appropriate. If describing a short-term job helps sell the applicant to the interviewer, then it's relevant. For recent college graduates, summer jobs are important and relevant to the graduate's total experience. An older applicant with extensive experience would probably omit summer jobs.

---

16 When a company asks you to complete an employment application form, an effective resume will suffice.

FALSE. Although it is tedious to complete an application form, refusal to do so will probably eliminate you from consideration. Companies need the completed form for personnel records, insurance and social security purposes, employment verifica-

tion, biographical information, references, and so
on.

Many enlightened firms don't ask you to fill out
the form until after they've interviewed you. But
most use it as a tool to evaluate applicants. There
are dozens of questions on standard application
forms that are seldom answered by individual resumes:

> Social Security number?
> How long have you lived at present
>   address?
> When will you be available for work?
> Person to be notified in case of emergency?
> That person's address and telephone
>   number.
> High school experience?

If a company you want to work for asks you to
supply such information, fill out the form completely and accurately.

---

17 Always list your salary on your resume.

FALSE. Never put your salary on the resume. The
place to state present salary or salary history is in
the cover letter accompanying the resume. Always
include your salary in the cover letter when the information is requested. If it's not requested, don't
include it.

18 *Always list references on your resume.*

FALSE. Never list your references on your resume. References are and should remain confidential.

Let's assume you've reached a point in the interviewing process when the employer asks, "We're interested in making you an offer, but we need to go through the formality of reference checks. What references do you wish us to contact?"

Let's assume further that you are interested in the offer. Your response should be, "Of course I will provide a list of references for you to contact. I'd like to call them first, however, to get their permission and to let them know to expect your call."

Then contact each reference you wish to use. Advise each one about the new job opportunity, what your responsibilities will be, why you left your last job, what the new company does, and any other relevant information that will enable the reference *to help sell you* to the new company. Then provide the name, address, and telephone number of each reference to your prospective employer.

19 *If you have just a couple of college courses and no degree, it's O.K. to state in your resume that you completed "two years" at a college or university.*

FALSE. Two courses do not constitute two years of college unless each course is a year of full-time study. There is never a need to lie in your resume, although nearly every resume contains at least one lie. If you have ever had occasion to read dozens of resumes, you'll recognize these common embellishments:

> No one has ever been out of work or between jobs. There are no work gaps.
>
> Everyone is in excellent health and has an exact, unfluctuating weight.
>
> Accomplishments and achievements at times warrant a Pulitzer Prize for fiction.
>
> The most recent job reads "1986 to present," despite the fact that the person has been unemployed for several months.

To lie in the resume or interview is risky since most items can be verified easily. Personnel departments can and do ask for evidence of past salary, educational transcripts, birth certificates, and social security records.

When you complete an application for employment, you'll be asked to sign the document to confirm that everything stated in it is true. If a falsehood is later discovered, that is grounds for immediate dismissal.

---

20 *It's a good idea to include height and weight in the personal section of the resume, particularly if the job hunter is tall.*

TRUE and FALSE. This is a free question because of my personal bias about what should and should not be contained in a resume. The question itself intimates a bias against short people. I feel height and weight are important only if you are applying for a job as a jockey, a defensive lineman, or a basketball player.

The EEOC believes a question about height and weight discriminates against women and Hispanics.

Although some jobs require a minimum height to operate a machine, the EEOC says platforms can resolve the problem.

No one in the history of mankind ever got a job offer through a resume alone—except professional football or basketball draftees or movie stars. Everyone else has to succeed in the interview. If you want your height and weight on the resume, go ahead and include it. You'll feel better. If you think that information is irrelevant, leave it out. You'll feel better.

---

21 *It's important to include your social security number on the resume to prove you've registered.*

FALSE. The only place you must write your social security number is on the application form. After you're employed, you'll also have to put your number on various tax and benefit forms. Most employers will request your social security card after employment to verify that the number is really yours. They may also request other documents after employment.

Putting your social security number on the resume just clutters it up. But, again, if it will make you feel better, go ahead and do it.

---

22 *If a job hunter doesn't have a typewriter, it's acceptable to write the cover letter in longhand, provided it's on personal stationery.*

FALSE. Rent a typewriter, borrow a typewriter, ask a friend or relative to type correspondence for you, or hire a typist. Sending a cover letter in long-hand may be expedient but it is not an acceptable business practice and should be avoided. All correspondence should be typed on personal stationery. Stationery is inexpensive. It should be ivory or white—no other colors. It should not have unusual type, script, or logos. Cute smile characters and animals are completely unacceptable. Note paper with "Have a nice day" or similar quotations is anathema.

Your letters are sales tools to help you obtain the final offer. Business correspondence requires business quality, style, and appearance. What you write, how you write it, and what you write it on reflects you, your attitude, your personality and education. Do it professionally, and carefully prepare and edit the finished product.

---

23 *Hiring a professional writer to prepare a resume is the way to make the best impression.*

FALSE. Most employment managers, who review hundreds of resumes each week, can identify the formula resume instantly—and will usually reject it.

If at all possible, you should prepare your own resume. Just as in the interview, you are the person best qualified to present your experience, achievements, and potential. Other people can help you edit and fine-tune your resume, but the heart of its content and style should be yours.

The career section of your local library has dozens of references to help you with the format of your resume. The content, however, must be original and fresh. Do it yourself.

---

24 *The resume is a sales tool, so the more self-praise and accomplishments it contains, the better it will be.*

FALSE. Self-praise is a judgment call and must be carefully assessed by the job hunter; too much is a turn-off, not enough is a mistake. Relevance is important; only someone applying for a job as a golf instructor, for example, should list an array of golf tournament victories.

In my collection of the worst resumes in the world is one from a marketing "expert" (who also put a picture of Pete Rose on his cover letter). Here are a few of his 30 achievements:

> Achievement #3   "The thrill of achievement really comes early! Got the lead in the kindergarden (sic) rendering of "Peter Rabbit" (May, 1932)."
>
> Achievement #10   "Every gentleman cannot possibly marry the loveliest girl in the world! I did! (October, 1950)."

It gets worse from there.

---

25 *Your reason for leaving each previous job must be stated in the resume.*

FALSE. Do not list reasons for leaving any job anywhere on the resume. You many describe your reason for leaving your present or most recent job in the cover letter that accompanies the resume. If you do, be sure to do it in a positive way. Do not say, "I got fired from my last job" or "I can't stand what I'm doing now, so I'm free to take anything" or "I can't get along with my boss."

Instead, talk about seeking better career opportunities, greater challenges, or a different career. Better still, leave the subject out of written correspondence; the interview is the best place to describe your new objectives.

A common question of job hunters is, "How do I tell a prospective employer I've been fired from my last job?" One solution is to say, "I realized that I could not succeed in that organization. Having discussed the matter with my boss, it was clear there were no other internal possibilities, so I'm looking at outside opportunities." You may feel that's a bit glossy, but it's better than "I was fired," and it's also a true statement. Few employers want to hear that you were fired because they have to verify the reasons for the termination. They'd much rather pick someone they like and let the personnel department worry about references.

ANSWERS 26-31
Networking

Networking is the key to a successful job search.

The basic tasks of a job search are fairly simple. Once you've figured out what kind of work you want to do, you need to know which companies might have such jobs and then make contact with the hiring authority. These tasks are also known as researching the job market and generating leads and interviews. Networking, or developing your personal contacts, is a great technique for finding out about market and industrial trends, and it is unsurpassed as a way to generate leads and interviews.

Networking is nothing more than asking the people you already know to help you find out about the job market and meet the people who are actually doing the hiring. Each adult you know has access to at least 300 people you do not know. Of course, a lot of them will not be able to do much in the way of helping you find a job. But if you start with, say, 20 or 30 people, and each of them tells you about 3 other people who may be able to help you, you've built a network of 60 to 90 contacts.

Mark S. Granovetter, a Harvard sociologist, reported to *Forbes* magazine that "informal contacts" account for almost *75 percent* of new jobs for professional and technical people, and ads yield another 10 percent or so.

To begin the networking process, draw up a list of all the possible contacts who can help you gain access to someone who can hire you for the job you want. Naturally, the first sources, the ones at the top of your list, will be people you know personally: friends, colleagues, former clients, classmates, relatives, acquaintances, customers, and club and church members. Just about everyone you know, whether or not he or she is employed, can generate contacts for you.

Don't forget to talk with your banker, lawyer, insurance agent, dentist, and other people who provide you with services. It is the nature of their business to know a lot of people who might help you in your search. Leave no stone unturned in your search for contacts. Go through your Christmas card list, alumni club list, and any other list you can think of.

On the average, it may take 10 to 15 contacts to generate 1 formal interview. It may take 5 or 10 of these formal interviews to generate 1 solid offer. And it may take 5 offers before you uncover the exact job situation you've been seeking. You may have to talk to a minimum of 250 people before you get the job you want. The maximum may be several hundred more.

Don't balk at talking to friends, acquaintances, and neighbors about your job search. In reality, you're asking for advice, not charity. Most of the people you'll contact will be willing to help you, if only you tell them how.

If I introduce you to my friend George at a major bank, he will get together with you as a favor to me. When you have your meeting with him, you will make a presentation about what you've done in your work, what you want to do, and you will ask for his advice, ideas, and opinions. That is an exploratory interview. As is true of any employment interview, you must make a successful sales presentation to get what you want. You must convince George that you are a winner and that you desire his help in your search.

The help the interviewer provides is usually in the form of suggestions to meet new people or to contact certain companies. I introduced you to George. Following your successful meeting, he introduces you to Tom, Dick, and Mary. Each of them provides additional leads. In this way, you spend most of your time interviewing, not staying at home waiting for the phone to ring or the mail to arrive.

A job doesn't have to be vacant in order for you to have a successful meeting with a hiring authority. If you convince an employer that you would make a good addition to his or her staff, the employer might create a job for you where none existed before. In this way, networking taps the "hidden job market."

To make the most of the networking technique, continually brush up on your interviewing skills. Remember, even when you're talking with an old friend, you are still conducting an exploratory interview. Don't treat it as casual conversation.

Begin networking with those people with whom you are most comfortable. Since many people know some information about you, there is a natural tendency not to mention that data. That's a mistake. You must present the same solid information about yourself to everyone so that you are certain to instruct each listener about the important facts they must know. To circumvent the embarrassment of being redundant, use the following ploy:

> "Mary, I know that you are aware of much
> about my background. But I'd like to ask
> you a favor. I'm going to make a
> presentation to you as I would to an
> absolute stranger. When we are

finished, I'd like you to critique what I've said."

This approach makes certain that you touch upon the highlights of your experience whether people are aware of those details or not. Remember, you are recruiting each person to help market you to the 300 people in their network whom you don't know.

This system and technique works. It is the most important bit of advice in this book.

---

26 "Networking" means talking to important people who have jobs.

FALSE. "Networking" means recruiting anyone to assist you in a job search. The saying, "It isn't what you know, it's whom you know that counts," is especially true in an employment search.

Networking is nothing more than asking people you already know to help you meet people you don't know. They, in turn, will help you find out about jobs that exist but aren't advertised or jobs that can be created. More important, they will lead you to the people who can hire you. Remember, you have access to dozens of people, and each of them has access to dozens more.

Don't exclude an old friend or classmate just because you haven't talked to him in years or because she lives out of state. Send a letter if a phone call doesn't work. Think of people in jobs you once held, former neighbors, or an old teacher. Sometimes a casual acquaintance or an old relationship can be more productive than the efforts of your closest friend.

27 *In networking, a wide array of people who provide services can become excellent sources of job leads.*

TRUE. Many job hunters have the mistaken impression that networking means talking only to people who have "important" jobs in their field of interest. In fact, networking is the process of recruiting people to help the job hunter examine the market. Everyone who works in a service capacity has access to people who may be excellent resources for the job hunter. One of my clients landed interviews with two company presidents by enlisting the aid of a waitress who had served them for years in a downtown restaurant.

When you're looking for work, talk with your insurance agent, broker, banker, druggist, doctor or dentist, travel agent, minister, priest, rabbi—in short, anyone you know who knows a lot of people. Give your contacts a brief rundown on your background, including what kind of work you've done and what you'd like to do. Be as specific as possible about how they can help you: do they know anything about XYZ Company or its director of marketing? Can they put you in touch with someone in the chemical engineering field? Do they have any other ideas?

If someone gives you a lead, follow up. Call Ms. Smith or Mr. Jones and let your contact know you appreciate his or her help. Few things are more irritating than to respond to a request for advice and then have your suggestion ignored.

28 *Companies that visit college placement offices to recruit seldom hire "C" students.*

FALSE. The grade point average of a student is only one of the variables reviewed. Technically, a "C" student is anyone between 2.0 and 2.9 on a 4.0 scale. But think of the difference between a 2.8 student who is in a work-study program, pays her own college expenses, and commutes daily, and the 2.0 student who isn't mature, doesn't work, and has no outside interests.

College recruiters do review grades and many other factors as well. These include:

> Ability to communicate
> Potential for growth
> Personality and appearance
> Ambitions
> Extracurricular activities
> Health
> Sense of humor
> Work experience
> Preparation for the interview

Keep in mind that the selection process is highly subjective. These other variables may also influence the recruiter:

> The student's family background
> Relatives or friends working for the
>   recruiter's company
> The student's military experience
> The student's references or sponsorship
> Previous employment with the company
> Fraternity or sorority relationships

One further word about campus interviewing. Here, as well as in the outside world, "whom you know" is important for the job hunter. Professor and employer references can open doors that grades alone can't budge.

---

29 The job search process requires about 20 hours of effort each week.

FALSE. Looking for a job is a full-time job in itself. If you are employed 40 hours a week, you'll have to conduct your job search during part of the 128 hours remaining. How much of that time you use is up to you.

If you are unemployed, you can spend at least 40 hours a week looking for a new job. Weekends and evenings can be used in networking among friends, relatives and neighbors. It seems unfair, but the amount of time you spend in a job search is not proportionate to the results you derive. One person may find success after four days of effort while another is still looking a year later.

Perhaps the best approach is to develop a sense of urgency; set the job search as your number one priority, and use all the time necessary to complete it. Twenty hours a week is rarely enough. On the other hand, 70 hours a week spent in a job search is as excessive as 70 hours a week spent in a job.

---

30 Professional directories are excellent sources of information for every job hunter.

TRUE. Professional directories contain information on products or services offered by various companies, volume of business, number of employees, office or branch locations, board members, officers and titles, and auditors. Four major sources of information with which every job hunter should be familiar are:

> *Standard and Poor's Register of Corporations, Directors, and Executives* (Standard and Poor's Publishing Co., 25 Broadway, New York, NY 10004).
>
> *Million Dollar Directory* (Dun & Bradstreet, Inc., 3 Century Dr., Parsippany, NJ 07054).
>
> *Thomas Register of American Manufacturers and Thomas Register Catalog File* (Thomas Publishing Co., One Penn Plaza, New York, NY 10119).
>
> *Moody's Complete Corporate Index* (Moody's Investor Service, 99 Church St., New York, NY 10007).

These directories are available in most public libraries. Larger libraries also contain dozens of other directories and guides to local resources that may come in handy. Keep in mind, however, that printed directories, even those that are regularly and conscientiously revised, go out of date as soon as someone listed in them gets promoted or changes companies. Always double-check a contact whose name you get from a directory or other printed resource. If necessary, call the company's switchboard to confirm a name or title.

31 *Any fraternity or alumni list has value to the job hunter, providing the hunter has been out of school less than four years.*

FALSE. Fraternity brothers and sorority sisters can be helpful for networking purposes no matter how long you've been out of school, or even if you never graduated. Alumni lists often reveal current business titles, companies, and addresses as well as home addresses and telephone numbers. They can be excellent resources if a job hunter wants to relocate to a different city or part of the country.

Try writing to every alumnus in the city or area where you want to relocate. Tell them that you would like to visit briefly to get some advice. Include a copy of your resume. State that you will call in a week or so to arrange a meeting during the time you will be in the area. In this way, a cluster of interviews can be arranged during the period. If there is a chapter in that city, you'll probably be able to stay at their facility at minimal expense.

Other organizations and fraternal groups can be equally helpful. Included in this segment are the Rotary, Elks, Moose, JayCees, and Kiwanis. Don't forget professional associations such as the American Chemical Society, Women in Association Management, American Society of Interior Designers, National Restaurant Association, League of Women Voters, or whatever groups coincide with your specific occupation or objective.

Most fraternities, sororities, and professional organizations publish a newsletter or magazine that can often direct their members to services and other resources available.

ANSWERS 32-45
Getting Interviews

We mentioned earlier that networking accounts for about 75 percent of all interviews that are obtained. Interviews can also be obtained through recruitment advertising (want ads), employment agencies, career counselors, executive search firms, direct contact with a company, or through part-time employment. A few comments about some of these sources may save you some time and lots of dollars.

Newspapers

Answering want ads is one of several tasks to be done in any job search, and generally among the least productive. According to *Forbes* magazine, only about 10 percent of professional and technical people find their jobs through want ads. Like any other long shot, however, answering want ads sometimes pays off. Be sure to check not only classified listings but also the larger display ads that appear in the Sunday business sections of major papers. These ads are usually for upper-level jobs.

Help-wanted listings generally come in two varieties: open advertisements and blind ads. An open ad is one in which the company identifies itself and lists an address. Your best bet is not to send a resume to a company that prints an open ad. Instead, you should try to identify the hiring authority and pull every string you can think of to arrange an interview directly.

The personnel department is in business to screen out applicants. Of the several hundred resumes that an open ad in a major newspaper is likely to attract, the personnel department will probably forward only a handful to the people who are actually doing the hiring. It's better for you to go to those people directly than to try to reach them by sending a piece of paper (your resume) to the personnel department.

Blind ads are run by companies that do not identify themselves because they do not want to acknowledge receipt of resumes. Since you don't know who the companies are, your only option in response to a blind ad is to send a resume. This is among the longest of long shots and usually pays off only if your qualifications are exactly suited to the position that's being advertised. Just remember that if you depend solely on ad responses, you're essentially conducting a passive search, waiting for the mail to arrive or the phone to ring. Passive searchers usually are unemployed a long time.

Newspaper business sections are useful not only for their want ads but also as sources of local business news and news about personnel changes. Learn to read between the lines. If an article announces that Big Bucks, Inc., has just acquired a new vice-president, chances are that he or she will be looking for staffers. If the new veep came to Big Bucks from another local company, obviously that company may have at least one vacancy, and possibly several.

Employment Agencies

The thousands of employment agencies that have succeeded through the years have done so by acting as intermediaries in the job market between buyers (companies with jobs open) and sellers (people who want jobs). An employment agency obtains a fee when a person it refers to a company is hired by the company. The fee may be paid by the company, but in some cases it is paid by the worker. Agencies that specialize in restaurant and domestic help, for example, often charge the worker a fee. Usually, the placement fee amounts to a certain percentage of the worker's annual salary.

A company that's looking for a secretary gains certain advantages by going to a reputable agency. It doesn't have to advertise or screen the hundreds of resumes that would probably pour in from even a small want ad in the Sunday newspapers. A good employment agency will send over only qualified applicants for interviews. Referrals are made quickly, and there is no cost to the company until it hires the secretary. For many companies, it's worth it to pay an agency fee to avoid the hassle of pre-screening dozens, if not hundreds, of applicants.

The value to the job seeker of using an employment agency depends on a number of factors, including the quality of the agency, the kind of work you're looking for, how much experience you have, and how broad your network of personal and business contacts is.

In general, an agency's loyalty will be to its source of income. Agencies are more interested in making placements than in seeing to it that applicants land jobs that are really fulfilling. An agency is likely to put pressure on its applicants to accept jobs they don't really want just so it can collect its fee. With certain exceptions (unless you're just starting out, new in town, or switching to a field in which you have no experience) an agency probably can't do much more for you than you could do for yourself in an imaginative and energetic job search. If a company has to pay a fee to hire you, you're at a disadvantage compared with applicants who are "free." Also, giving an employment agency your resume could be a serious mistake if you're trying to conduct a confidential job search.

On the other hand, a good agency can help its candidates develop a strategy and prepare them for employment interviews. This training can be very valuable to people who are inexperienced in job-hunting techniques. Agency pros know the market, screen well, and provide sound advice. A secretary who tries to investigate the market on his or her own will take up to six times longer to get the "right" job than someone who uses a quality agency.

Most importantly, be sure to read the contract thoroughly, including all the fine print, before you sign it. If you have any questions or if there's something you don't understand, don't be afraid to ask. It's your right. Make sure you know who is responsible for paying the fee and what the fee is. Remember that in some cases an agency's application form is also the contract.

The advantage to the agency of a successful placement (besides the fee) is repeat business. After two or three referrals work out well, an employment agency can generally count on receiving future listings of company vacancies.

Career Consultants

If you open the employment section of the Sunday newspaper or the national edition of *The Wall Street Journal*, you'll see several ads for career consultants (also known as career counselors or private out-placement consultants). The ads are generally directed to "executives" earning yearly salaries between $20,000 and $300,000. Some ads suggest that the consultants have access to jobs that are not listed elsewhere. Others claim, "We do all the work." Most have branch offices throughout the country.

Career consultants vary greatly in the kind and quality of the services they provide. Some may offer a single service, such as vocational testing or resume preparation. Others coach every aspect of the job search and stay with you until you accept an offer. The fees vary just as broadly and range from one hundred to several thousand dollars. You, not your potential employer, pay the fee.

A qualified career consultant can be a real asset to your job search. But no consultant can get you a job. Only you can do that. You are the one who will participate in the interview, and you are the one who must convince the employer to hire you. A consultant can help you focus on an objective, develop a resume, research the job market, decide on a strategy, and train in interviewing techniques. But you can't send a consultant to interview in your place. It just doesn't work that way.

Don't retain a career consultant if you think that the fee will buy you a job. The only reason you should consider a consultant is that you've exhausted all the other resources we've suggested here and still feel you need expert and personalized help with one or more aspects of the job search. The key to choosing a career consultant is knowing what you need and verifying that the consultant can provide it.

Check references. A reputable firm will gladly provide them. Before you sign anything, ask to meet the consultant who will actually provide the services you want. What are his or her credentials? How long has the consultant been practicing? Who are the firm's corporate clients?

Read the contract carefully before you sign it. Does the contract put the consultant's promises in writing? Has the consultant told you about pro-

viding services that are not specified in the contract? What does the firm promise? What do you
have to promise? Are all fees and costs spelled out?
What provisions are made for refunds? For how
long a time can you use the firm's or the consultant's services? Be sure to do some comparison
shopping before you select a consultant.

Executive Search Firms

An executive search firm is one that is compen-
sated by a company to locate a person with specific
qualifications that meet a precisely defined employment need. Most reputable executive search
firms belong to an organization called the Association of Executive Recruiting Consultants (AERC).
The association publishes a code of ethics for its
membership.

A search firm never works on a contingency basis. Only employment agencies do that. The usual
fee for a search assignment is 30 percent of the
salary of the person to be hired, plus out-of-pocket
expenses. These are billed on a monthly basis.
During hard times, most companies forego retain-
ing search firms because it's so expensive.

It's difficult to get an appointment to see a search
specialist. Executive search consultants have only
their time to sell. If a specialist spends time with
you, he or she can't bill that time to a client. If you
can use your personal contacts to meet a search
professional, however, by all means do so. Executive specialists know the market and can be very
helpful in providing advice and leads.

Search firms receive dozens of unsolicited resumes every day. They seldom acknowledge receipt
and usually retain only a small portion for future
search needs or business development. They really
can't afford to file and store them all. Sending your
resume to every search firm in a given metropoli-
tan area will be useful only if one firm coincident-

ally has a search assignment to find someone with exactly your background and qualifications. It's a long shot, similar to answering blind want ads.

---

32 *The personnel department does all the hiring and firing, so that's the first place to contact to get an interview.*

FALSE. Most personnel departments do not have the authority to hire. The individual department manager is generally the hiring authority, that is, the person who extends the offer. The personnel department then processes the offer.

The employment manager is responsible for attracting applicants. This is done through referrals, advertising, employment agencies, search firms, and other available resources. Then the screening process begins. The task is to reduce the hundreds of applicants, interview the remainder in person, and then reject most and accept a few for further consideration by the hiring authority. Only two or three people actually get the opportunity to make a sales presentation to the person doing the hiring.

The conclusion is obvious: try to contact the hiring authority without going through the personnel department. You'll have to see personnel people eventually, but it's more effective not to begin there.

One final point. The employment manager's job is to fill "authorized requisitions," that is, company-approved openings. The employment manager usually cannot create an opening when an outstanding applicant is available. The hiring authority, on the other hand, sometimes thinks, "If the right person ever comes along, I'm going to get into this new service or product line. I'll just add another box to the organization chart and drop a memo to personnel."

---

33 *Most employers are inundated with unsolicited resumes. It makes sense to be a bit assertive and show up in person to request an interview rather than to send paper.*

FALSE. There is little doubt that employers are inundated with unsolicited resumes. But showing up at a company without an appointment may reflect poor judgment rather than assertiveness.

It is presumptuous to assume that busy people will drop everything to spend time with a job hunter. Sometimes people will; but most times the job hunter will be directed to the personnel department and asked to complete an application. Usually, about three weeks later, the job seeker receives a #4 form letter stating that the application will be kept on file should an opening develop in the future.

Avoid that whole process; save yourself time, expense, and anxiety. Find out from your own sources (or the company telephone operator) who heads the department where the opening exists. Contact that person by mail or phone and try to set up an appointment. This approach may not always work. But it beats being one of 400 application forms sitting on a desk in the personnel department.

34 *The easiest part of the job search is the interview.*

TRUE. The interview should go smoothly, providing the applicant is properly prepared. The interview is a conversation, a sales presentation, and an exchange of information. The subject of the conversation is primarily the person being interviewed—the job hunter—*you!* Since you are the world's leading authority on you, no one is more qualified to discuss you. The interview should be the easiest part of the search. But it seldom is.

Most people lack experience in interviewing. Furthermore, we've been conditioned since childhood that it's not nice to brag or boast. That may be true at dinner parties. But the goal of the employment interview, whether it's a formal session or an informal chat over coffee, is to convince the interviewer that you have the ability, experience, personality, maturity, and other characteristics required to do a good job, and to enlist the interviewer's help in getting you that job.

In an informal networking interview, you'll talk with friends, relatives, and acquaintances. These are the people who most want to help you. They can't do so, however, unless they know who you are, what you've done, what you want to do, and, most importantly, how they can help you. An employer wants the same information. If you don't provide it, or provide only parts of it, someone else gets the offer.

Spend some time rehearsing your presentation. Use a tape recorder and answer the typical questions found in any book on interviewing. Critique yourself. Then try your presentation out on a couple of friends. The more often you interview, the better you get, and the easier it becomes to sell yourself in the interview.

35 *Sending 100 resumes to 100 different company presidents is certain to generate at least 10 interviews.*

FALSE. Volume mailings are good for the economy: they require paper, printing, postage, envelopes, delivery, routing, reading, responses, more stationery, postage, and redelivery. They are also good for the job hunter's morale. Surely, something has to come from so much work and expense. The end result, however, is usually no more than one to three interviews per hundred contacts. The response rate may exceed 50 percent, but 98 percent of the responses will be negative. The job hunter who sits back and waits for the mail to arrive or the phone to ring is conducting a passive search. Passive searches tend to be unproductive.

The active search requires personal contact—lots of formal and informal meetings to discover what is available in the market and to sell the job hunter's skills. Remember, 93 percent of the jobs that exist are never advertised. Networking is the key to discovering them.

36 *The old adage, "See someone who knows someone," is the heart of networking, the best technique for getting interviews.*

TRUE. This is one of the most important points in this book. Networking is the foremost method of generating interviews.

Networking is nothing more than asking the people you already know to help you find out about the job market and meet the people who are actually doing the hiring. Each adult you know has access to at least 300 people you do not know. Of course, some will not be able to do much in the way of helping you find a job. But if you start with, say, 20 or 30 people, and each of them tells you about 3 other people who may be able to help you, you've built a network of 60 to 90 contacts.

Statistics show that networking, or using informal contacts, accounts for almost 75 percent of all successful job searches. Agencies find about 9 percent of new jobs for professional and technical people, and employment advertisements yield another 10 percent or so.

---

37 *A guaranteed way to generate employment interviews is to run an advertisement describing skills, experience, and salary.*

FALSE. In 30 years of experience, I've never met anyone who got a job that way. If answering a blind ad is a long shot, running a blind ad for yourself is an even longer shot, and certainly a more expensive one.

Granted, running an ad is a different approach. But so is wearing a sandwich board stating "I want a job" and parading up and down Main Street. Most readers will only wonder why the person isn't using more conventional techniques and assume that something must be wrong if he or she has to advertise.

38 *Employment agencies can get you a good job.*

FALSE. Only you can succeed in an interview and be offered a job. Employment agencies, executive search firms, or career counselors cannot do that for you.

An effective employment agency can, however, be very helpful in the job search. A good agency counselor can identify markets for your skills and advise you about unique company needs. The agency may also have corporate clients who will interview you even though there are no listed openings.

A good counselor can provide valuable information on interviewing techniques, resume or application preparation, follow-up contact, references, salary negotiations, and so on. But the agency can't get you the job. Only you can do that.

One of the most common mistakes made by a job hunter is to assume that registering with several agencies is all that is required to succeed in a search. That's as naive an assumption as the idea that sending 700 resumes to 700 company presidents will get you the offer you want.

39 *A school's placement office can assist in the search if the job hunter is a graduate of that school.*

TRUE. This is an important source of free help that most job hunters overlook. The school placement office is available to all students and graduates of the school. Most offices have a separate service for alumni placement, giving the experienced job hunter access to employers who are looking for experienced people. The placement director usually is familiar with the employment market, salary ranges, job changes, transfers, and leads that can help in networking.

It's usually worth your while to call or visit your alumni placement office to explain your background and the position you're seeking. (Be sure to bring several copies of your resume for them to circulate.) Although most school placement directors are overworked, they generally have time for an alumni who may later be in a position to hire recent graduates.

---

40 Employment agencies work on a contingency basis, so they really do not benefit the job hunter.

FALSE. A contingency fee means the agency will be paid only if their referral is hired. Sometimes the job hunter is liable for the fee, but most often the hiring company is responsible.

Most agencies provide some benefit to the job hunter, though some do not. The contingency fee may make an agency reluctant to work with job hunters whose objectives don't match the agency's listings. Less scrupulous agencies may refer the job hunter to jobs that are outside his or her interest.

---

41 "Headhunter" refers to employment agencies, executive search firms, and career counselors.

FALSE. The term "headhunter" is used only for executive search consultants who are retained by corporations to seek people for specific positions.

Frequently, the person sought has already been identified; the search consultant then has the delicate task of approaching the candidate and attracting him or her to the new position. Another term for a headhunter is "pirate."

The public often confuses executive search consultants and employment agency counselors. Agency counselors, sometimes known as "flesh peddlers," get their fee only if a referral is hired. Search consultants are paid whether a referral is hired or not; they don't work on a contingency basis.

Lately, a new breed of counselors has developed. This is the "career consultant," who offers services to the job hunter for a fee. A few unethical career consultants make false promises to the job hunter and then do not deliver; they are called "vultures" because they prey on naive, unemployed, or desperate people who believe paying a fee will guarantee a better job.

Caveat emptor. Executive search firms, employment agencies, and career consulting firms can perform a superb service for the job hunter. But it is up to the job hunter to be selective in choosing a firm and services to meet his or her needs.

---

42 Employment agency contracts are all identical since they are state-regulated.

FALSE. Each state's requirements are different, and every employment agency contract has unique clauses and conditions. A job hunter should carefully review an employment agency contract before signing it.

> What is the fee?
> Who pays it?

What are the services provided by the
agency?
For how long is the contract binding?
What happens if either party defaults?
What are the job hunter's responsibilities
after signing the contract?

All professional employment agencies require a
contract. The job hunter should also be professional and take the time to understand the sub-
tleties of engaging an agency. Professional agencies
are regulated by each state's Department of Labor.
That's the proper mediator, should there be any
contract disputes.

---

43 *Answering help-wanted ads is an integral
part of any job search but is usually not
too productive.*

TRUE. There are too many people answering ads.
It is not uncommon for a blind advertisement in a
regional section of The Wall Street Journal to receive 600 responses. According to Forbes magazine,
only about 10 percent of professional and technical
people find their jobs through want ads.

---

44 *In answering an ad, it's best not to include a salary requirement or present
salary even if the ad requests salary
data.*

FALSE. The reader of your resume and cover letter wants to know if your salary requirement falls
within the range of the position advertised. Almost

69

all positions have a salary minimum, midpoint, and maximum range. Employers prefer to hire new employees at or below the midpoint of the range.

Many people feel that by not including salary, they increase their chances for consideration for jobs slightly below their present or past salary. That doesn't happen. By omitting salary from the cover letter, the applicant unwittingly eliminates himself or herself from consideration. A reader with a stack of hundreds of responses to plow through simply is not going to take the time to call you for salary information. The reader will choose other applicants to interview.

A person's salary is a reflection of market value for a set of specific responsibilities. Including a realistic salary requirement in the cover letter will save you time by eliminating you from consideration for a job that is totally inappropriate.

---

45 Companies that run blind advertisements (do not reveal their identity) do so because they don't want their employees to know they are advertising.

FALSE. Companies run blind ads to avoid responding to a barrage of unsolicited phone calls and personal visits. The blind ad generally elicits a high response, though it eliminates people who never answer such ads for fear of jeopardizing their present job.

Job hunters should answer any ad that truly interests them. They should realize, however, that the probability of getting a response from a blind ad is less than 2 percent, and the probability of generating an interview is even less. Answering help-wanted ads can be part of your arsenal, but it's a passive long shot. Personal networking is active and the most effective technique for generating interviews.

ANSWERS 46-79
Interviewing

Networking and interviewing go hand-in-hand; all the contacts in the world won't do you any good if you don't handle yourself well in an interview. No two interviews are ever identical, except that you always have the same goal in mind: to convince the person to whom you're talking that he or she should help you find a job or hire you personally. An interview is also an exchange of information. But you should never treat it as you would a casual conversation, even if the "interviewer" is an old friend.

Whether you're talking to the housewife next door about her brother-in-law who knows someone you want to meet or going through a final, formal interview with a multi-national corporation, you are essentially making a sales presentation—in this case, selling yourself. Your goal is to convince the interviewer that you have the ability, experience, personality, maturity, and other characteristics required to do a good job and to enlist the interviewer's help in getting you that job.

In an informal interview you'll be talking first to friends and acquaintances. Most of the people you'll be talking to will want to help you. But they need to know who you are, what you've done, what you want to do, and, what's more, how they can help you.

To prepare for an interview, first perfect what we like to call the "five-minute resume." Start by giving a rough description, not too detailed, of what you're doing now (or did on your last job) so that while you're telling your story the listener won't be distracted by wondering how it's going to end.

Then go all the way back to the beginning—not of your career, but your life. Talk about where you were born, where you grew up, what your folks did, whether or not they're still living, what your brothers and sisters do, and so on. Then trace your educational background briefly, and, finally, outline your work history from your first job to your latest.

"What!" say many of our clients. "Drag my PARENTS into this? Talk about my crazy BROTHER and the neighborhood where we grew up?"

Yes, indeed. You want to draw the listener into your story, to make him or her interested enough in you to work for you in your search. You want the interviewer to know not only who you are and what you have achieved but also what you are capable of. You also want to establish things in common with the listener. The more you have in common, the harder your listener will work for you.

The typical applicant begins a presentation with something like, "I graduated from school in June, nineteen-whatever, and went to work for so-and-so." Our task in this book is to teach you how not to be typical. Our experience has convinced us that the way to get a job offer is to be different from the rest of the applicants. You shouldn't eliminate the first 20 years of your life when someone asks you about your background! That's the period that shaped your basic values and personality.

Neither should you spend too much time on your personal history. A minute or two is just about right. Then go on to narrate your work history. You'll have from three to eight minutes to accomplish this. Most exploratory interviews, and many initial employment interviews, are limited to half an hour. If you can give an oral resume in five to ten minutes, you have roughly twenty minutes left to find out what you want to know (more on that shortly).

A word about your work history. In the oral resume you want especially to emphasize your successes and accomplishments in each job. That will take some practice. We are not accustomed to talking about ourselves positively. From childhood, we're conditioned that it's not nice to brag. Well, we are here to tell you that if you don't do it in the interview, you won't get the offer.

We repeat: the interview is a sales presentation. It's the heart of your job search, your effort to market yourself. In an exploratory interview the listener will be asking, "Should I help this person?" In a formal interview, the employer will be asking, "Should I hire this person?" In either case the answer will be "yes" only if you make a successful presentation, if you convince the interviewer that you're worth the effort.

So the first step in preparing for any interview, formal or informal, is to practice your five-minute resume. Go through it out loud enough times so that you're comfortable delivering it. Then work with a tape recorder and critique yourself. Try it out on a couple of friends.

When you're preparing for a formal employment interview, do your homework on the company. This advice is merely common sense. But it's surprising how many candidates will ask an interviewer, "What does this company do?" Don't be one of them. Before you go in for an employment interview, find out everything you can about the company—its history, organization, products and services, and growth expectations. Get hold of the company's annual report, catalogs, and brochures.

In an exploratory, or informal, interview most of the people you'll talk with will want to help you. But they need to know how. After you've outlined your personal and work history, ask your contact how he or she thinks your experience fits into today's market. What companies should you visit? Specifically, what people should you contact?

When someone gives you advice or a recommendation to call someone else, do it! Few things can be more irritating than to provide free counsel to someone who then ignores it. If your contact suggests that you call Helen Smith, call her!

In a formal employment interview there are several typical questions you can expect to encounter, though not necessarily in the following order. Most often heard is, "Tell me about yourself." That is your cue for the five-minute resume.

Other typical questions include:

Why do you want to change jobs?

What kind of job are you looking for now?

What are your long-range objectives?

What are your salary requirements?

When could you be available to start here?

Tell me about your present company.

What kind of manager are you?

How would you describe yourself?

What are your strengths and weaknesses?

Describe your present boss.

Whom should I talk to about your performance?

Are you open to relocation?

How long have you been looking for a new job?

Why are you interested in this company? (This is your golden opportunity to show the interviewer that you've done your homework on the company.)

Practice your answers to these questions before you go in for the interview. Anticipate other questions you might be asked, and develop answers for them. In general, keep your responses positive. Never volunteer a negative about yourself, another company, or a former employer.

The interviewer will apply your responses to the questions he or she really wants answered:

Does the applicant have the ability to do the job?

Can he or she manage people?

How does he or she relate to people?

What kind of person is this? A leader? A follower?

What strengths does he or she have that we need?

Why the number of job changes so far?

Where is he or she weak?

How did the applicant contribute to present and past companies?

What are his or her ambitions? Are they realistic?

Is he or she too soft or too tough on subordinates?

What is this person's standard of values?

Does he or she have growth potential?

Is there a health problem anywhere?

What is the nature of the "chemistry" between us?

What will the department manager think of this applicant as opposed to the others?

The interview should not be a one-sided affair, however. Questions that you should ask the interviewer are equally important in this exchange of information. For example, you have to know about the job, the company, and the people in your future employment situation. It's necessary to use your judgment to determine how and when to ask questions in an interview. But without the answers, it will be next to impossible for you to make a sound decision if you receive an offer. Some of the questions you want answered are:

What are the job's responsibilities?

What is the company's recent history? Its current objectives?

What is the company's market position? Where are its plants located? What distribution systems does it use? To whom will I report? What's his or her background?

Why is the job available?

Where does the job lead?

What about travel arrangements?

Where is the job located?

Are there any housing, school, or community problems that will develop as a result of this job?

What is the salary range?

What is the detailed benefit picture?

What is the company's relocation policy?

When will an offer or decision be made?

What references will be required?

When would I have to start?

> What is the personality of the company?
> Do the job and company fit my plan for
>   what I want to do now?
> What's the next step?

Many job seekers experience a kind of euphoria after a good interview. Under the impression that a job offer is imminent, a candidate may discontinue the search. That is a serious mistake. The decision may take weeks or may not be made at all. On the average, about six weeks elapse between the time a person makes initial contact with a company and receives a final answer. If you let up on the search, you will prolong it. Maintain a constant sense of urgency. Get on with the next interview. Your search isn't over until an offer is accepted and you actually begin the new job.

Always follow up an interview with correspondence. The purpose of the letter is to supplement the sales presentation you made. Thank the interviewer for his or her time and hospitality. Express interest in the position (ask for the order). Then mention three additional points to sell yourself further. Highlight how your specific experience or knowledge is directly applicable to the company's immediate needs. Try to establish a date by which a decision will be made.

---

46 *Military experience is an important part of a person's life and should be thoroughly discussed in an employment interview.*

TRUE. The interview is a sales presentation to convince the interviewer that the applicant's personality, experience, and potential will contribute to the employer's profitability. Military experience can be an asset. Let's say John Doe graduated from college and entered Officer Candidate School in the U.S. Army. As an officer in the infantry, he became a platoon leader after completing Airborne and Ranger training. He experienced combat in Vietnam before being released from active duty and finished his military obligation in the Reserves. What conclusions might an interviewer form about John Doe? Some of the following deductions might be made:

> He is a leader.
> This person is disciplined.
> He accepts responsibility.
> He is a risk-taker.
> He is probably dependable.
> He is hard-working.
> He is able to set goals and achieve them.

These conclusions could work in John's favor in an interview. Keep in mind that experience in transportation, distribution, mechanics, materials control, engineering, navigation, flight training, and thousands of other military occupation specialties can be applied to civilian endeavors. Ignoring military experience in an interview wastes an excellent opportunity to add sales points to the overall presentation.

47 Which of the following questions is illegal and cannot be asked by a prospective employer?

A ☐ Have you ever been convicted of a crime?

B ☐ Why were you fired from your last job?

C ☐ Are you currently receiving unemployment compensation?

D ☐ What was your father's occupation?

"A" is the answer closest to being "illegal" (see question number 81). The only time this question should be asked during an employment interview is when the company is doing certain government work that requires a security clearance.

48 An employment interview is a sales presentation by the applicant, so the job hunter must sell experience, personality, potential, and strengths.

TRUE. Communicating your personality, potential, and strengths in an interview is far more difficult than communicating specific historical experience. Nevertheless, that is the job hunter's task. It is not the interviewer's job to draw out this information; indeed, most interviewer's don't know how to do so.

Simply put, if you don't sell yourself in the interview, another candidate will get the offer. And you can't sell yourself without preparation.

49 *"Are you open to relocation?" is a common interview question. If the job hunter doesn't want to move, the best answer is "No!"*

FALSE. By saying no, you may eliminate yourself from consideration for a job that presently doesn't require relocation but may with future promotions. The purpose of the interview is to get an offer. It's far better to answer the question with some reservation:

Q. "Are you open to relocation?"

A. "Depending upon the job, I certainly would consider it."

The above answer is not a lie. It simply says, "I really need more information and an offer to decide if relocation makes sense." The door stays open, and the interview continues.

---

50 *When asked the very common question, "What are your strengths and weaknesses?" it's a good idea to be modest about strengths and perfectly honest about limitations.*

FALSE. The job hunter must present his or her strengths in a straight-forward manner. We have all been conditioned since childhood to be modest and not to boast. But stating your strengths in a competitive employment interview is not bragging—*it is absolutely essential.*

Because you aren't used to discussing your own strengths, it may be worthwhile to rehearse your answer. For example, "I've been told that my greatest strength is my personality. I'm well read,

81

articulate, comfortable before groups, and get along with all kinds of people. I'm creative, resourceful, hard working. I get things done on time and within budget."

"Previous performance appraisals have stated that I'm dependable, work well under pressure, am flexible, and demonstrate good leadership traits. I particularly enjoy selling because of my persuasive abilities. And as you can tell, I'm modest and have a sense of humor."

Never claim positive traits unless you actually possess them. If you don't have a mind for details, it's foolish to lie and suggest that you do. On the other hand, don't be afraid to discuss any positive quality you do possess.

What about the negatives? A general rule in interviewing is never to volunteer a negative comment about yourself, another person, or a company. What do you do, then, when you're asked, "What are your weaknesses, limitations, or areas that need improvement?" Sharing negative information can only give the interviewer a reason for rejection. I recommend volunteering something that will be socially acceptable and not self-demeaning. Instead of saying, "I don't like routine" (every job has some routine), say, "I wish I were fluent in French or Spanish." Only one negative is necessary. Other socially acceptable responses are:

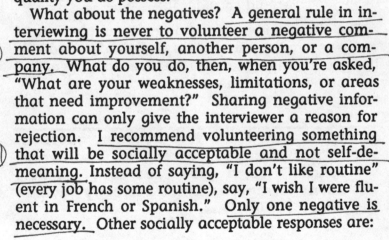

> I'd like to read all the magazines that I subscribe to.
>
> I wish I could lower my golf handicap from 19 to 15.
>
> I really should write my relatives more often.
>
> I wish I could spend more time with my children.

51 *When an interviewer asks what you do in your spare time, he or she really wants to know if you have bad habits.*

FALSE. The only reason this silly question is in this book is because some people don't have the foggiest idea how to answer it. When I've asked people what they do in their spare time, over the years I've collected the following incredible replies:

> Nothing.
> What spare time?
> Watch TV.
> Sleep.
> Hang out.
> I don't know.
> Work a second job.

If you were an interviewer, what judgments or conclusions would you draw about the person who provided any of those responses?

Now consider some other possible answers:

> ✳ Play golf, tennis, swim, run.
> Engage in family activities.
> ✳ Participate in church activities.
> I like to garden, work on the car, fix things around the house.
> I write short stories.
> ✳ I enjoy reading.
> ✳ I take adult education courses.
> I participate in community activities, Rotary, Lions, Jaycees, whatever.
> I collect stamps, coins, art.

We all do something that improves the mind, body, or spirit, but we may not place much emphasis on the activity. To make an effective presentation in the interview, be sure you identify those activities and enthusiastically describe them. The listener will be excited and interested only if you are excited and interesting.

---

52 When the subject of salary comes up during the interview, the job seeker should automatically ask for a salary 15 percent higher than the present or last salary.

FALSE. Most jobs have a salary range. Employers prefer to hire people at or below the midpoint of the range in order to allow room for raises in the future and to protect the company's internal salary structure.

By requesting an "automatic" 15 percent, you may be putting yourself above or below that range. The best strategy is to tell the interviewer your present or most recent salary and let the employer make his/her best offer. Some employers may simply ask, "What will it take to get you to work with us?" Even in this case, it's risky to set a specific figure. An increase of 10 percent is usually enough to attract a new employee. If relocation is required, 15 percent to 25 percent is not uncommon, in addition to covering relocation expenses.

Salary is an important part of your strategy for a new job, and you should know the minimum salary that is acceptable to you. This will, of course, depend upon all other variables of the job. For example, if there is a performance and salary review three months after starting, the job hunter might accept a lower salary than for a job that offers a review only after one year.

Other factors to consider are the job benefits, your career path, responsibilities, company growth, the people you'll work with, the management, and the products or services the company provides. Salary is important, but it seldom is the most important of these factors.

---

53 If a job seeker talks about background, grade school and high school activities should never be mentioned.

FALSE. Personal background should include a brief review of where you grew up, your parents' occupations, something about your brothers and sisters, and where you went to grade school and high school.

What possible relevance does this have to your getting a job at age 30, 40, or 50? The few minutes it takes to talk about your youth is worthwhile, though few people take the time to do so and even fewer understand the value of doing so.

As a sales presentation, the interview will succeed only if the interviewer feels comfortable with the applicant and has a few things, people, or experiences in common. For example, if you both went to the same school or grew up in the same part of the country, have mutual friends, served in the military, came from large families, or were only children, these common factors enhance your probability of "making the cut."

Certain high school honors are also worth mentioning. Being class president or a member of a state championship team or a National Merit Scholar reveals another of your positive qualities. Most listeners will be interested in these details and will evaluate them as points in your favor.

---

54 *Ten or 15 years after college, your grade point average is of no interest to the interviewer.*

TRUE. Someone interviewing an applicant who has been out of school for a long time is interested in knowing if you graduated, what school you attended, and what your major was but seldom cares about your grade point average. (Recent graduates are an exception.)

Nevertheless, exceptional performance is worth mentioning. If you graduated *cum laude* or completed four years with an A-minus average, this should be included in the interview and on your resume.

When I am asked about my high school experience, I always mention that I graduated fourth in my class. Seldom does anyone ask how many students were in the class. (There were seven.)

---

55 *The decision to hire or not to hire is generally made in the first five minutes of the interview.*

FALSE. This is one of the most persistent myths about the employment process. First impressions are important, but the decision to hire requires sufficient time to review technical ability, experience, personality, and potential. People are also capable of rethinking their first impression.

Remember, the interview is generally an unusual experience for both parties. The applicant and the interviewer may be anxious, ill prepared, or uncomfortable. As the conversation continues and they discover common experiences or needs, the tone of the interview can change. As they say in baseball, "It ain't over 'til it's over."

---

56 An interviewer has a right to ask an applicant's net worth.

TRUE. The net worth of a person is his or her total assets minus total liabilities. The question—along with current annual salary—may be asked by companies in the banking, insurance, brokerage, or financial industries. Executive search consultants in particular like to use the question.

Why do they ask? The answer would have less relevance in a younger applicant, but it may show thrift, investment savvy, and perhaps a certain maturity about financial matters.

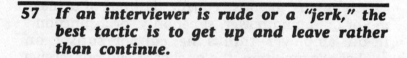

---

57 If an interviewer is rude or a "jerk," the best tactic is to get up and leave rather than continue.

FALSE. The purpose of the interview is to make the "cut" and get the offer. You can't do this if you leave in the middle of the interview. After you receive the offer, you may question working for a company whose representative is rude, but at least you've succeeded in the interview and met your objective.

It's necessary to be patient with certain interviewers. Your time and expense have already been invested. Leaving may make you feel better, but it would be a lost opportunity and a mistake. There will be other instances, after you're employed, when you'll have to deal with rude customers or a client who is a "jerk." Your ability to deal with such a situation in an interview could be a preview of what lies ahead.

---

58 When asked to describe your strengths, it's good to use words such as "aggressive," "assertive," and "ambitious."

FALSE. The interviewer judges which adjectives are positive or negative. It's up to the job hunter to choose words that are not threatening to the interviewer. "Assertive," for example, means "to assert" or "to stand with assurance, confidence, or force." That may be fine for a salesperson but disastrous for a counselor or administrator.

"Aggressive" means "tending toward aggression," which really means "an unprovoked offensive attack, invasion, or the like." It suggests hostility— hardly an asset.

"Ambitious" means "eagerly desirous of achieving or obtaining power, superiority, or distinction." If an employer thinks he cannot satisfy an applicant's ambition, the applicant will not receive the offer.

---

59 If asked, "Tell me about your spouse," the best answer is to advise the interviewer politely that the question is illegal.

FALSE. Doing so could irritate the interviewer, create a negative impression, and violate the strategy of the interview—which is to get the offer. The best approach is to ignore the illegality of the question and tell the interviewer about your spouse. Describing a husband or wife supplements the sales presentation and enhances your image.

What's more, your spouse's assets—personality, occupation, abilities, interests—can add to your value.

The manner in which a person describes a spouse sometimes reveals the quality of a marriage. When I ask men who have been married more than 20 years, "Tell me about your wife," a typical response is, "We've been married 26 years. She's a good cook, very supportive of my career, active in the church, and has a good sense of humor." Then, there's a long silence because he can't think of anything else to say. When I point out that he didn't even mention her name, there is generally some embarrassment. He has described her as a possession rather than a person. What does that reveal about him? (Also see Question 81.)

---

60 It's ill advised to ask an applicant, "What branch of the military did you serve in?"

TRUE. Although we've indicated earlier that there are no "illegal" questions, this is a question to be avoided unless the job specifically requires someone from the army or navy. Each applicant must be asked the same questions, and the employer must evaluate answers according to the uniform guidelines for employment procedures outlined by the Equal Employment Opportunity Commission.

Why is this question ill advised? The Commission suggests that it may have a disparate impact on one group or another and thus could potentially discriminate on the basis of race or sex. It could also discriminate against people who have a military liability particularly when draft laws apply.

61 "How's your health?" is an illegal question.

FALSE. A prospective employer has the right to know the general nature of an applicant's health. Most organizations will provide a doctor to complete a thorough physical examination. Passing the physical exam is usually a prerequisite for employment. It is the doctor who determines the state of the applicant's health and his or her physical and emotional ability to meet the demands of the position.

Don't be alarmed if an employment application requests detailed information about your medical history. Above all, do not lie about your health. Often, people who have had cancer, epilepsy, sight or hearing problems, a heart attack, or a stroke fear they will be rejected out of hand. Most doctors, however, will know if your medical history will affect your ability to meet the requirements of a given job. If it does, most likely you shouldn't be doing that job for your own protection. (Also see Question 84.)

62 It's best to show up for an interview at least 20 to 30 minutes early.

FALSE. Arriving a few minutes early is perfectly acceptable, but being announced 20 to 30 minutes earlier than you're expected is a mistake. The interviewer expects the applicant at the appointed time, not before or after. It's advisable to allow enough time for traffic, unfamiliarity with the area, parking, or weather problems. Plan to stop in the restroom before your appointment to check your appearance and help nature relieve your normal anxiety. Be on time and arrive relaxed, composed, and ready to sell yourself.

---

63 *To prepare for employment interviews, companies always thoroughly read the applicant's resume and sometimes make reference checks before the interview.*

FALSE. Few interviewers thoroughly prepare for an interview, and seldom do they check references beforehand. They know that doing so without the applicant's permission may jeopardize the confidentiality of the application.

Since the interviewer seldom prepares, the applicant must take responsibility for bringing out the relevant information in the interview. This is where the sales presentation is so important. (Review the answer to Question 48.)

If the job hunter assumes the resume will speak for itself, he/she loses an opportunity to communicate personality, experience, and a wealth of specific information directly to the employer. It's a mistake to let the interviewer control the interview to such an extent that there is no dialogue—the applicant must play an extremely active role. Just as a salesperson would be dominant in a sales presentation, the job hunter must orchestrate the interview.

To do this effectively, the job hunter should prepare an eight-to-ten-minute life review, highlighting each major aspect of his/her background. (Yes, it can be done in ten minutes.) A tape recorder can be an enormous help in doing this.

Here's a beginning: "Thanks for seeing me, Mr. Brown. In the interest of time, perhaps it would be beneficial if I gave you a broad-brush review of my background. Then we'd have time to discuss specific questions. Would that be all right? [Of course.] Well, as you know, I'm presently doing corporate outplacement and individual career counseling. Originally, I'm from Chicago..." Then the job hunter presents the heart of what the interviewer wants to know.

---

64 ***College honors, self-supported tuition, fraternity or sorority offices held, and the like have little place in the interview.***

FALSE. All of that information has value and adds to the interviewer's positive image of the applicant. Putting yourself through college is an achievement. That doesn't mean that an applicant whose education was financed by parents is less desirable; it simply shows the responsibility and independence of the self-supported student.

Offices held in extracurricular activities usually indicate commitment, leadership, above-average participation, people orientation, and a willingness to assume additional responsibility. (On the other hand, of course, the interviewer may be biased against fraternities.) If you have information about your college experience that is positive, by all means volunteer it in the interview. It will almost certainly add to your overall assessment.

---

65 ***To ease tension and establish rapport with the interviewer in the first few minutes, it's a good idea to tell a joke or two.***

FALSE. "A funny thing happened to me on the way to the interview" is not the mature way to begin. Establishing rapport early in the interview is important, but telling jokes isn't the way to do it.

Generally, comments about the weather, traffic, or other light subjects give you a chance to put each other at ease. If you're networking, begin the conversation with a reference to the person you both know: "Lisa Sullivan felt that you were the ideal person to provide some of the advice I need to begin my search." The response will probably be, "How is Lisa?" or "How do you know Lisa?"

The interview is a serious matter, but it need not be solemn. The job hunter should smile when appropriate and not conceal a sense of humor, but the interview doesn't require a stand-up comic performance.

---

66 Smoking or chewing gum during an interview may cause the interviewer to reject an applicant.

TRUE. Most interviewers will form a negative judgment about applicants who smoke, chew gum, or exhibit other idiosyncratic behavior. Even if the applicant is not rejected outright, he or she may be perceived as immature, inconsiderate, nervous, inexperienced, self-centered, careless, or poorly disciplined.

Do not smoke or ask permission to smoke during the interview unless the interviewer is smoking. Never chew gum in an interview.

---

67 *Common sense dictates that people should dress conservatively for an interview, avoiding gaudy clothing or extreme styles.*

TRUE. There isn't too much to add, except to say that while appearance alone won't get you a job (unless you're a model), it can certainly cost you one.

---

68 *A winning smile and a firm handshake can make the difference between "winning" or "losing" in an interview.*

FALSE. The content of the interview determines if an offer will be made or not. A weak smile and handshake won't help, but these are minor points. Overall demeanor, presence, grooming, preparation for the interview, knowledge of the company, background, listening skills, enthusiasm, personality, ability to communicate, and dozens of other combined factors determine who will get an offer.

---

69 *Before the employment interview, the applicant should do some homework on the company. It's poor form to ask the interviewer, "What does your company do?"*

TRUE. Lack of preparation shows the interviewer that the job hunter isn't interested, is careless, lazy, or simply not too bright.

By studying the company's size, products, services, organization, and recent experience, the job hunter can determine how he or she would fit in.

Before the interview, try to discover how you could contribute to the company's profitability. Get a copy of the company's annual report as well as its catalogs and brochures. Use the resources suggested in Answer 30 to research the company's structure, officers and titles, and so on.

---

70 *A supply of resumes, a contact list, a calendar, and a job log are the briefcase contents every job seeker should carry to every interview.*

TRUE. The contact list enables the job hunter to make additional appointments and use the time available between interviews to the best advantage. The calendar controls the time available.

The job log is really a journal of the entire search. The job hunter records every contact made during the search, whether it be a brief conversation, a phone call, or an interview. The log should contain the following data:

1. The date the contact was made.
2. The name, address, and telephone number of the contact and the contact's company.
3. The disposition of the contact, that is, what happened as a result of the meeting. If a phone call resulted in an appointment for an interview, the date of the interview should be recorded in the log and the calendar. If a hiring authority suggested by a contact is out of town for three days, that should be noted, too, so that the hiring authority can be called at the appropriate time.
4. Any tax-deductible expenses incurred during your search.

When dealing with hundreds of people, which is normal in a three-month search, the job hunter needs a way to keep track of leads and make sure that no information falls through the cracks. The job log functions as a control device.

The log is also an audit of your own search performance. If you make only two or three entries in the log in the course of a day, you're probably waiting for the mailman to arrive or the phone to ring instead of actively working at the search. Fifteen or more daily entries that result in four or five interviews is a good day's output.

---

71 *What a person says in the interview determines whether he or she gets the offer.*

FALSE. What is said in the interview is extremely important, but the interview is not the sole determinant for getting the offer. The applicant must have the ability to do the job that is available as well as the experience and personality to compete successfully against other applicants for the job.

---

72 *When the interviewer says, "Tell me about yourself," the interviewer really wants to know only about your personality.*

FALSE. The statement, "Tell me about yourself" can be translated:

> Why should I hire you?
> Why are you here?
> What is your background and ability?

Who are you?
The floor is yours, go!

Seize the opportunity to present a 5- to 10-minute verbal resume of your background, education, job experience, personality, achievements, accomplishments, career direction, family situation, salary, current job situation and reason for changing it. Before you go to any interview, practice this oral sales presentation. Spend a minute or two on your personal history, and devote the rest of the presentation to your work and professional background.

Make the presentation a couple of times in front of the mirror. Then work with a tape recorder and critique yourself. Try out your presentation on a couple of friends. Do enough homework on the company before the interview so that you can show the interviewer specifically how you can contribute to the organization. The resources suggested in the answer to Question 30 will help in your research. So will the company's annual report and sales brochures.

---

73 *If there are a few applicants for one position, the person with the best technical qualifications generally gets the offer.*

FALSE. If there are a few people to choose from, technical qualifications are just one factor among many. The interviewer usually selects the person with whom he or she is most comfortable. Personality, appearance, age, chemistry, personal background, sex, size, shape, and color all influence choice. Although there are laws against unfair selection practices, people still choose candidates who have similar values, were in the same branch of the military, are Yankees fans, or went to the same school.

The more a candidate has in common with the interviewer, the greater the probability of surviving the first cut and eventually receiving an offer. The interviewer cannot ask certain questions about personal background, but the job hunter can volunteer such information. In fact, the job hunter's task is to reveal as much as necessary about personal background. Avoid the common mistake of restricting the interview conversation to technical qualifications alone.

---

74 *Most employers are willing to spend time with anyone interested in getting a job in their company.*

TRUE. But not their own time. Employers prefer to refer any inquiries to the personnel department. If a job hunter calls Mr. Bowen, a company manager, to ask for an interview, the inquiry will generally be routed elsewhere or screened by phone. It's best to use a third-party referral to meet a hiring authority.

Try to avoid absolutely cold calls. If the job hunter uses a reference who is known to Mr. Bowen, a personal interview will probably be arranged as a favor to the third party. Then you can say to the personnel person, "Mr. Bowen suggested I contact you to present my credentials to ABC Company. When would it be convenient for you to spend some time with me?" In most cases, since personnel is a service organization, the department will arrange an interview as a service to Mr. Bowen.

75 Anytime the national unemployment rate exceeds 9 percent, it's almost impossible to get a job.

FALSE. The national unemployment rate is often used as an excuse by job hunters who are not successful in their search. Recently, the country suffered from the highest unemployment rate in decades—but people were still being hired, still switching jobs, even when more than one out of ten people were out of work.

It's understandable why some job hunters will say, "There are no jobs" or "I can't get a job if I'm over 50!" It's easier to blame conditions beyond your control than to admit your own failure. But failure isn't necessary. With proper preparation, you can land the job you want despite age, salary, education, or the state of the economy. The only variable you can't control is how long it takes.

The Labor Department estimates that the average search takes 19 weeks. Of the 150 people who used our outplacement service during the heart of a recession, the average search took three months. One client, aged 56, had looked for a job on his own for four months, relying solely on classified ads and letter writing. Needless to say, his passive efforts didn't work. Frustrated, he sought counsel and was taught how to network. He began active searching and two months later accepted one of two offers that met his needs.

Remember, a 10 percent unemployment rate means 90 percent of the labor force is working.

76 Pre-employment polygraph (lie-detector) tests are against the law.

TRUE and FALSE. The Employee Polygraph Protection Act of 1988 prohibits most private employers from requesting or requiring an employee or prospective employee from taking polygraph examinations or disciplining those who refuse to take such examinations. Federal, state, and local government employees are exempt from the Act.

The Congressional Office of Technology Assessment estimates that 2,000,000 polygraph exams were conducted in 1987, 90 percent by private employers. About 85 percent of that number would be banned under the new law.

Federal contractors engaged in security, intelligence, or top-secret projects are exempt. Also exempt are firms that need security guards to protect money and pharmaceutical companies that employ people to make, distribute, or disperse drugs.

77 It's best to look for another job while you are still employed.

TRUE. It's better to be employed than unemployed. Of course, there are problems associated with conducting a job search while employed:

> The search is generally restricted to evenings and weekends.
>
> There are ethical issues involved in interviewing with another firm when you are being paid by your current employer.

Your current employer may discover your dissatisfaction and encourage you to leave or simply fire you.

The search may be restricted to passive methods such as answering ads or sending letters. Often, the job hunter receives a single offer which he/she must react to without a chance to investigate alternatives.

However, the advantages of looking for another job while employed outweigh the disadvantages:

The job hunter is under no time constraint or pressure for income and can conduct the search as long as he/she wishes.

The employed job hunter avoids the bias against the unemployed.

The job hunter's recent position may improve, thus eliminating the need to switch jobs.

The job hunter's superior might leave, thus creating a new opportunity with the current employer.

---

78 *If a job hunter wants to work in another city, it's best to move there first and then start looking.*

FALSE. During the last recession, thousands of job hunters who headed for Dallas, Houston, and Atlanta were severely disappointed. Most returned to their point of departure still unemployed, broke, and more discouraged than ever.

Developing interviews in another city requires careful planning and research. Network sources can be found in directories such as Dun & Bradstreet's *Million Dollar Directory*, the *Thomas Register*, the city's Chamber of Commerce membership directory, the *Yellow Pages*, trade and professional journals, newsletters (many of which have job listings), and of course, through personal contacts. Subscribing to the local newspaper will enable the job hunter to see what companies are doing, who is hiring, what the cost of living is, and so on.

One approach is to identify companies you wish to interview and contact the person who would hire you. Tell him or her that you are going to be in the city and would like to meet briefly to explore employment possibilities. Although there may be no specific openings in the company, if you use a third party referral (a mutual friend or acquaintance), you should be able to arrange a meeting.

As long as you are in the city, try to arrange a cluster of interviews. Most employers will invite you to visit if it costs them nothing, and each interview may generate new leads. Relocate only after an offer has been extended and accepted. It's less expensive and much less stressful.

---

79 *Most employment managers consider it a breach of ethics for an employee to look for another job on company time.*

TRUE and FALSE. It is a breach of ethics for a job hunter to seek employment elsewhere on company time. Many people do so anyway since employment managers prefer to conduct interviews during normal business hours. A job hunter has two choices: to take paid vacation or to interview during personal time off without pay. Although few people lose sleep over the issue, interviews can be arranged at breakfast, lunch, dinner, weekends, and in the evening. Preliminary interviews can be arranged on personal time, and the more extensive company interviews can be arranged during vacation time off.

ANSWERS 80-100
Other Items

In 30 years of employment counseling experience, I'm still surprised by what people say and do not say about themselves during an interview. In the sixties, I believe the Equal Employment Opportunity Commission did a disservice to corporate America by creating some strange rules of interviewing. As usual, companies reacted to EEOC requirements so strongly that the employment interview became something of a monster.

Employment managers across the country demanded that their company interviews adopt a "sterility of purpose" so strong that fear overcame common sense. That situation still exists in some companies. People—both interviewer and job hunter, freeze at the thought of such an encounter. "Can I ask if the candidate has a family?" "Can I volunteer the fact that I have a family?" The number of such questions have people so concerned that it's a problem even when it really should be viewed as humorous.

In the following Quiz answers, we want to point out how common sense should prevail in the EEOC items, reference arrangements, and job-offer tactics. Indeed, throughout the Quiz you must have concluded by now that many of the questions presented have multiple answers, depending upon additional variables. My purpose in writing this book is to enable each reader to become more confident in a job search by learning that there are many myths about job hunting and that the ominous task is far easier than imagined.

I guarantee that if you apply the principles we have outlined in this little book, your search will be successfully concluded quicker, with less pain and fewer mistakes. More importantly, you'll never be afraid to leave a bad job or a job that was good but changed.

PERSONAL

---

80 *During the interview, it's best to avoid any personal information about family background, marriage, children, or the like.*

FALSE. Personnel professionals insist that an applicant's "personal life" has nothing to do with the job and therefore has no place in the interview. They are over-reacting to EEOC requirements. If you were hiring someone to work for your company, wouldn't you be interested in the person's background, personality, education, and early experience?

An interviewer shouldn't ask you about your marital status, but you can certainly volunteer the information. No one will ever ask, "How many children do you have and what are their ages?" but if you have a family and fail to talk about them, you're missing an opportunity to supplement your presentation with valuable information about yourself.

The most common mistake made by applicants is to ignore the first 21 years of life. Experience shows that job hunters who volunteer personal information are more successful in interviews than those who do not. We repeat that it makes excellent sales sense to mention briefly where you were born, grew up, what your folks did, what your brothers and sisters do, etc. These are common denominators with the interviewer.

You want to draw the listener into your story— not just discuss your technical accomplishments and job history but tell who you are and what is important to you, what you've done and can do. Talk about yourself as completely as time allows. This doesn't mean describing your alcoholic Uncle Charlie or your eccentric brother-in-law. Use common sense to develop a brief presentation of the personal information you think is important to share.

---

81 *It is illegal for an employer to ask an applicant about marital status or religious background.*

FALSE. According to an Equal Employment Opportunity Commission compliance manager, there is no such thing as an "illegal" question. The issue is the purpose of asking the question. If the purpose is to discriminate against one group or another and/or there is no business necessity for asking the question, a charge of discrimination can be made. If the question, "Are you Roman Catholic?" is asked in a pre-employment interview for a sales position in a department store, it would have no relevance to the position. Religious preference doesn't predict sales success, and there is no business necessity for the information. It would be assumed the purpose of the question was to screen out either Catholic applicants or non-Catholics.

Let's assume the same question were asked to fill the position of Religious Education Director in the Diocese of Joliet, Illinois. It would be perfectly acceptable since an applicant must be Roman Catholic to meet the objectives of the job.

Usually when an "illegal" question is asked about marital status, religion, age, height and weight, or other sensitive areas, it reflects an interviewer's incompetence more than an intention to discriminate. The best tactic is probably to answer the question, pursue and receive the offer, then try to determine if the interviewer is indeed biased or just stupid. In either case, the job hunter may not want to work for such an organization.

Some questions are so obvious that the intention is clear. "Who watches the children when you work?" "I noticed your engagement ring; what are your family plans?" or, "What is your relationship with your ex-wife?" are classics. Whether or not to file charges depends on the time and other resources you can devote to a lawsuit.

---

82 If a job hunter is divorced, an employer can ask who has custody of the children.

FALSE. The question may not be asked during the employment interview, but it is permissible after employment if necessary for insurance purposes. This is one of the questions that rightfully infuriates women. The interviewer is really trying to determine if a woman will miss work or be late if her children are ill or require attention. Men are never asked the question; it generally reflects inherent discriminatory attitudes on the part of the employer.

83 *Most personnel people regard divorce as a sign of failure, so never volunteer that information in a resume or interview.*

TRUE. The bias isn't restricted to personnel people. Although most people won't admit it, despite the awesome number of divorces today, divorce is regarded as a sign of failure. If you were divorced (the thinking goes), you must have done something wrong, failed in some way.

In our experience in career counseling, the only time divorce has been considered an asset was in the case of an auditor for a large accounting firm. As a divorced man, he was free to travel for the client company 95 percent of the time, making him more desirable than an applicant with a family.

84 *Always include the statement, "In excellent health," in the personal section of your resume no matter what your health condition is.*

FALSE. See Question 61. Leave the health statement off the resume completely. It is assumed by the reader of the resume that everyone is in excellent health until proven otherwise.

85 *Beards and long hair on men are still perceived negatively, even if the beard is handsomely trimmed.*

TRUE. Most of the business world considers beards and long hair a sign of rebellion. Seldom will you see beards on men in insurance, banking, investment banking, or manufacturing management. Beards are more common in advertising, the arts, print and broadcast media, market research, research and development, education, and certain branches of government.

My advice to a job hunter who has a beard or long hair is to conform to the norm in his field until after a job offer is obtained. The same advice applies to men with pierced ears and earrings.

---

86 *Anyone with graying hair who is looking for a new job had best color or dye it to look younger.*

FALSE. Although the strategy worked very well for former President Reagan it isn't necessary for job hunters to dye their hair. If a person wants to look younger and feels good about such cosmetic changes, fine. But the key to getting a job offer is succeeding in the interview, not having darker, thicker, or more hair.

---

87 *People over 50, women, blacks, and the unemployed are generally discriminated against in the employment process.*

TRUE. Despite the advances that have been made in federal, state, and local laws, employers still discriminate, if not as overtly as they have in the past.

> Young is preferred to old.
> Male is preferred to female.
> White is preferred to all other races.

Employed applicants are preferred over
unemployed.

For older, female, non-white, or unemployed applicants, the challenge of selling themselves and
convincing prospective employers that their experience and potential will enhance the company's
profitability is greater. If discrimination in employment is blatant with a particular employer, le-
gal recourse is available to every citizen. If one has
the energy and resources both to continue the job
search and to file suit, so much the better.

---

88 Most people in the work force are college graduates.

FALSE. The U.S. Department of Labor confirmed
that in March, 1983, there were 20.2 million workers aged 25-64 who had completed four or more
years of college. That represented only 24 percent
of the work force, though it was up from 16 percent
ten years earlier.

If you are interested in statistics, here are some
other figures gathered by Thomas J. Moore of the
Chicago *Sun-Times* Washington Bureau:

In 1965 about 12 of every 100 high school
graduates completed college. But 1980
that figure had increased to 19 out of
every 100.

The educational system is producing
almost twice as many college graduates
as there are college-level jobs.

More than 40 percent of college graduates
enter jobs in which most of their fellow
workers don't have a degree.

Many take white collar jobs that previously went to high school graduates.

The supply and demand curve of college grads suggests that most positions really do not require a college education. Many job hunters claim they can't get a job because they don't have a college degree. The fact is, three out of four workers do not. The odds favor the high school graduate.

REFERENCES

---

89 *Reference checks are still an important element of the job search; references should be carefully prepared.*

TRUE. Today, the process of checking personal references has become fairly automated. The personnel department may simply send a form letter to an applicant's previous employers to verify dates of employment, title, salary, reason for leaving, and eligibility for rehire. The form letter is generally sent after employment is offered and is placed in the employee's personnel file.

Certain professionals, however, may check references very thoroughly before employment. By telephone or in person, they might ask references about an applicant's performance, personality, strengths, weaknesses, managerial ability, contributions, and accomplishments, and real reasons for leaving. Such interviews can be very probing.

The job hunter should carefully select references who will be able to help sell him or her to a prospective employer. These references should be used only if the job hunter is interested in a specific company and job and the company is interested in making an offer. At that point, the company should request references and the job hunter should reply, "I'm certainly interested in the position and would be glad to provide personal references. I would like to contact them first, however, to tell them you'll be calling and why."

The job hunter then briefs each reference about the company, the job, his or her reason for leaving the most recent employer, and any other information that will *help the reference sell the job hunter.* Don't supply a prospective employer with names, addresses, phone numbers, and titles of people who are not expecting a reference call.

References are valuable and should not be abused by excessive or unnecessary calls. References are perishable items. Treat them carefully.

---

90 *Employers really don't have the time to verify previous employment or educational background and seldom do so.*

FALSE. Many do not, but most have a very consistent policy of verifying information on the application for employment form.

Ever since the *Washington Post* incident in which a reporter fabricated a story that was awarded a Pulitzer Prize, employers have been nervous about forgoing thorough reference checks.

Certain organizations hire background investigators. Banks and most large companies verify education and past employment for everyone hired. Certain defense-connected firms require a security clearance, which may warrant investigation by the F.B.I.

Most employment application forms state that falsifying information is grounds for dismissal. It never benefits the job hunter to lie on a resume, employment form, or during an interview.

91 *If your references include important people—authors, judges, sports figures—it's
a good idea to include them on your resume to make it more impressive.*

FALSE. Although we said earlier that the resume
can contain anything that makes you feel better
(because resumes are not as important as most
people think), we also said that the resume should
never contain negative information. Listing important people as references is "name dropping,"
and most people have an aversion to name-drop-
pers.

References, as we have said, should never be
placed in the resume. If you wish to use an important person as a reference, be certain that person
really knows you well enough to speak about your
technical ability, personality, and career background. It would be disastrous to list a famous figure who, when contacted, says, "Barbara who?
Never heard of her!" What is said about you is
more important than who says it.

92 *Personnel departments cannot legally
verify salaries of former employees, so
the job hunter can claim any salary
he/she likes.*

FALSE. Some personnel departments will protect
confidential information about past employees, including salary information. Other personnel departments have no such policy and are free to confirm or deny salary inquiries.

Never lie about compensation. A prospective
employer can easily ask you to substantiate your
current or past salary simply by asking to see a pay

receipt or a W-2 form. Once you've been caught in a lie or exaggeration, your credibility can seldom be regained.

OFFERS

93 Formal employment contracts are usually provided only to senior executives.

TRUE. When a middle-management or senior non-exempt person loses a job for the first time, he or she may have a strong desire to have a contract the next time in order to reduce the likelihood of termination or at least provide a lucrative severance arrangement. Unfortunately, such contracts are usually restricted to top level officers and senior executives. If it is possible to negotiate a contract, by all means consider doing so. Remember, though, that if a contract has a termination date, it may not be renewed despite your performance. The "protection" of a contract still does not guarantee security.

94 An employer extending a job offer expects to wait at least three weeks for an answer.

FALSE. Every employer thinks his/her offer is so fabulous that any applicant would accept it on the spot. You shouldn't, of course: but neither should you take three weeks to answer.

It requires time to review an offer carefully and to compare its terms to your initial objectives. A week or two is a reasonable time in which to do this and to pull in any outstanding irons you have in the fire. If the employer refuses to wait a week or two, without exceptional reasons, it's a pretty good indication of the conditions under which you'll be working.

Most working professionals will want to give their current employer two to four weeks' notice. It's the current employer's option to shorten that period if it's beneficial to him or her.

How does one analyze an offer? Thoroughly. A job involves much more than a title and base salary. Be sure you understand what your responsibilities will be, what benefits you'll receive besides salary (insurance, vacation, profit sharing, training, tuition reimbursement, and the like), how much overtime is demanded (and whether you'll be paid for it), how much travel is required, who your superior will be, how many people you'll be supervising, and what the potential for advancement is.

For many positions, especially those requiring several years' experience, it's appropriate to ask for an offer in writing. Such a document should specify the position's title, responsibilities, reporting relationship, and compensation, and should include a statement of company benefits.

At the very least, before you make a decision, be sure to obtain a copy of the company's personnel manual, detailing benefits and policies. It's not a bad idea to try to assign a dollar value to benefits to help you evaluate the offer.

95 *A formal offer of employment is a letter outlining title, salary, reporting relationships, benefits, and other important aspects of the job. Without such a letter, there is no formal offer.*

TRUE. An informal offer is a verbal commitment from the hiring authority to the applicant. The job hunter should always try to get the offer in writing, if possible, so there is no mistake about the conditions of the offer. Formal, written offers are usually limited to employees who are exempt from the Fair Labor Standards Act and are not paid overtime. They are referred to as "exempt" employees. "Non-exempt" or "hourly" personnel generally do not receive formal employment offers. But they can still request a letter from the personnel officer.

All too often, job hunters wrongly interpret an interviewer's enthusiastic response as an offer. Most professionals concur that an offer isn't an offer until it's in writing.

96 *Temporary work often leads to permanent employment, so it makes sense to accept a temporary job as soon as possible.*

FALSE. The job hunter's objective and financial circumstances determine whether or not a temporary job is appropriate. While temporary work may sometimes lead to permanent employment, it takes the job hunter out of the search for the duration of the engagement. It can also affect the sense of urgency and cost the job hunter opportunities for a higher salary and more permanent responsibilities. If financial circumstances permit, the job hunter should look for work full time. On the other hand, if money is needed to meet immediate obligations, temporary work can be a bridge between unemployment and the ideal job. In either case, a temporary position should not be a job hunter's first objective.

---

97 Getting a good score on a civil service test guarantees a job offer.

FALSE. A good score is beneficial and very important in applying for a civil service job, but there are additional criteria to be considered, including:

> Citizenship
> Experience
> Education
> Available openings
> Competition
> Government experience
> Minority status
> Veteran status

A good civil service test grade no more guarantees a job offer than a college degree.

---

98 A company can fire an employee who lied about anything on the employment application form.

TRUE, if the employee signed the form, which usually has a statement like this:

> I understand that willful misrepresentation of any information supplied on this

form is adequate cause for removing me
from consideration for employment or
immediate discharge from employment.

Signature_____

Date signed_____

**99 Sometimes the hiring authority in a de-
partment, if sufficiently impressed by the
candidate, can create a new job.**

TRUE. That's why the job hunter can ignore
personnel's declaration, "We have no jobs." Personnel people are seldom in a position to create an
opening. A manager, however, can.

Perhaps the manager has thought, "If the right
person ever comes along, I'll get into this project or
that service, or get rid of Smith." If there is an opportunity for a manager to increase profitability by
hiring you, the manager certainly wants to hear
about it. If the manager thinks you're a winner but
can't hire you now, he or she may do so in the future or may refer you to one of his resources now.
This is elementary networking—or should appear
so to you by now.

**100 "Overqualified" is a rejection excuse that
really means "too old."**

FALSE. When an employer tells an applicant that
he or she is overqualified, the employer usually
means: "You have more experience than this job
requires. You won't learn very much, you'll get
bored or disinterested, you'll be unproductive, and
you'll probably begin looking for another job fairly
soon. I'll have to spend time and money to hire and

train a replacement, and my experience tells me it's easier to reject you now."

Sometimes "overqualified" means an applicant is too expensive. Occasionally, it is used as an excuse for rejecting an applicant on the grounds of age. In most cases it is to the job hunter's advantage not to pursue a job for which he or she is deemed overqualified unless a solid case can be made for age discrimination.

In summary, here are a few other major points to remember:

> The first step in a job search is to develop an objective.
>
> Resumes don't get jobs.
>
> Networking is the best way to generate interviews.
>
> Succeeding in the interview gets the offer.
>
> The interview is a sales presentation.
>
> Do your homework on a company before you go in for an interview.
>
> Reveal enough personal information in the interview to give the hiring authority a sense of who you are and what you can accomplish.
>
> References can help sell you to an employer.
>
> With proper preparation, you can get the job you're qualified for.
>
> The only uncontrollable variable is how long it will take.

I hope this exam will stimulate your interest sufficiently to apply the techniques and principles outlined in these pages. Now that you've read this far, wait a few days and take the test again—we've reproduced it in the following pages. Your score the second time should reflect how ready you are to start and succeed in your search.

REPEAT QUIZ
Find Out How Much You've Learned

1. Take the test.
2. Score yourself.
3. Read the answers.
4. Take the test again (it's repeated in the back of the book).
5. Score yourself again, and see how much you've progressed.

1 Most people are able to find a job in a week or two. If it takes longer than a month, something is terribly wrong.

☐ **TRUE**   ☐ **FALSE**

2 The first paragraph of your resume should contain a thorough explanation of your employment objective.

☐ **TRUE**   ☐ **FALSE**

3 The federal, state, and local governments are still excellent employers.

☐ **TRUE**   ☐ **FALSE**

4 During an economic recession, recent graduates have a better chance for jobs if they have an MBA.

    ☐ **TRUE**   ☐ **FALSE**

5 Being unemployed is an embarrassment, so if you lost your last job, it's best to keep it to yourself.

    ☐ **TRUE**   ☐ **FALSE**

6 It's better to be unemployed than underemployed.

    ☐ **TRUE**   ☐ **FALSE**

7 Someone who loses a job or gets fired should take a few weeks off before starting a search in order to sort things out.

    ☐ **TRUE**   ☐ **FALSE**

8 Maintaining a positive outlook about job hunting has very little value if the national unemployment rate exceeds 9 percent or the local rate exceeds 14 percent.

    ☐ **TRUE**   ☐ **FALSE**

9 There is no such thing as a perfectly secure job.

    ☐ **TRUE**   ☐ **FALSE**

10 Companies don't hire people. People hire people.

    ☐ **TRUE**   ☐ **FALSE**

11 The first step in any job search is to develop an outstanding resume.

☐ **TRUE**   ☐ **FALSE**

12 The length of any resume should be:

A ☐ One page

B ☐ Two pages

C ☐ Three pages

D ☐ As long as needed

13 If the job hunter is particularly attractive, it's a good idea to include a picture with the resume.

☐ **TRUE**   ☐ **FALSE**

14 Any time a job hunter answers an advertisement, a cover letter must accompany the resume.

☐ **TRUE**   ☐ **FALSE**

15 It's important to include every job you ever held when writing a resume.

☐ **TRUE**   ☐ **FALSE**

16 When a company asks you to complete an employment application form, an effective resume will suffice.

☐ **TRUE**   ☐ **FALSE**

17 Always list your salary on your resume.

☐ **TRUE**   ☐ **FALSE**

18 Always list references on your resume.

☐ TRUE   ☐ FALSE

19 If you have just a couple of college courses and no degree, it's O.K. to state in your resume that you completed "two years" at a college or university.

☐ TRUE   ☐ FALSE

20 It's a good idea to include height and weight in the personal section of the resume, particularly if the job hunter is tall.

☐ TRUE   ☐ FALSE

21 It's important to include your social security number on the resume to prove you've registered.

☐ TRUE   ☐ FALSE

22 If the job hunter doesn't have a typewriter, it's acceptable to write the cover letter in longhand, provided it's on personal stationery.

☐ TRUE   ☐ FALSE

23 Hiring a professional writer to prepare a resume is the way to make the best impression.

☐ TRUE   ☐ FALSE

24 The resume is a sales tool, so the more self-praise and accomplishments it contains, the better it will be.

☐ TRUE   ☐ FALSE

25 Your reason for leaving each previous job must be stated in the resume.

☐ **TRUE** ☐ **FALSE**

26 "Networking" means talking to important people who have jobs.

☐ **TRUE** ☐ **FALSE**

27 In networking, a wide array of people who provide services can become excellent sources of job leads.

☐ **TRUE** ☐ **FALSE**

28 Companies that visit college placement offices to recruit seldom hire "C" students.

☐ **TRUE** ☐ **FALSE**

29 The job search process requires about 20 hours of effort each week.

☐ **TRUE** ☐ **FALSE**

30 Professional directories are excellent sources of information for every job hunter.

☐ **TRUE** ☐ **FALSE**

31 Any fraternity or alumni list has value to the job hunter, providing the hunter has been out of school less than four years.

☐ **TRUE** ☐ **FALSE**

32 The personnel department does all the hiring and firing, so that's the first place to contact to get an interview.

☐ **TRUE** ☐ **FALSE**

33 Most employers are inundated with unsolicited resumes. It makes sense to be a bit assertive and show up in person to request an interview rather than to send paper.

☐ TRUE   ☐ FALSE

34 The easiest part of the job search is the interview.

☐ TRUE   ☐ FALSE

35 Sending 100 resumes to 100 different company presidents is certain to generate at least 10 interviews.

☐ TRUE   ☐ FALSE

36 The old adage, "See someone who knows someone," is the heart of networking, the best technique for getting interviews.

☐ TRUE   ☐ FALSE

37 A guaranteed way to generate employment interviews is to run an advertisement describing skills, experience, and salary.

☐ TRUE   ☐ FALSE

38 Employment agencies can get you a good job.

☐ TRUE   ☐ FALSE

39 A school's placement office can assist in the search if the job hunter is a graduate of that school.

☐ TRUE   ☐ FALSE

40 Employment agencies work on a contingency basis, so they really do not benefit the job hunter.

☐ **TRUE**   ☐ **FALSE**

41 "Headhunter" refers to employment agencies, executive search firms, and career counselors.

☐ **TRUE**   ☐ **FALSE**

42 Employment agency contracts are all identical since they are state-regulated.

☐ **TRUE**   ☐ **FALSE**

43 Answering help-wanted ads is an integral part of any job search but is usually not too productive.

☐ **TRUE**   ☐ **FALSE**

44 In answering an ad, it's best not to include a salary requirement or present salary even if the ad requests salary data.

☐ **TRUE**   ☐ **FALSE**

45 Companies that run blind advertisements (do not reveal their identity) do so because they don't want their employees to know they are advertising.

☐ **TRUE**   ☐ **FALSE**

46 Military experience is an important part of a person's life and should be thoroughly discussed in an employment interview.

☐ **TRUE**   ☐ **FALSE**

47 Which of the following questions is illegal and cannot be asked by a prospective employer?

    A ☐ Have you ever been convicted of a crime?

    B ☐ Why were you fired from your last job?

    C ☐ Are you currently receiving unemployment compensation?

    D ☐ What was your father's occupation?

48 An employment interview is a sales presentation by the applicant, so the job hunter must sell experience, personality, potential, and strengths.

    ☐ TRUE   ☐ FALSE

49 "Are you open to relocation?" is a common interview question. If the job hunter doesn't want to move, the best answer is "No!"

    ☐ TRUE   ☐ FALSE

50 When asked the very common question, "What are your strengths and weaknesses?" it's a good idea to be modest about strengths and perfectly honest about limitations.

    ☐ TRUE   ☐ FALSE

51 When an interviewer asks what you do in your spare time, he or she really wants to know if you have bad habits.

☐ **TRUE**   ☐ **FALSE**

52 When the subject of salary comes up during the interview the job seeker should automatically ask for a salary 15 percent higher than the present or last salary.

☐ **TRUE**   ☐ **FALSE**

53 If a job seeker talks about background, grade school and high school activities should never be mentioned.

☐ **TRUE**   ☐ **FALSE**

54 Ten or 15 years after college, your grade point average is of no interest to the interviewer.

☐ **TRUE**   ☐ **FALSE**

55 The decision to hire or not to hire is generally made in the first five minutes of the interview.

☐ **TRUE**   ☐ **FALSE**

56 An interviewer has a right to ask an applicant's net worth.

☐ **TRUE**   ☐ **FALSE**

57 If an interviewer is rude or a "jerk," the best tactic is to get up and leave rather than continue.

☐ **TRUE**   ☐ **FALSE**

58 When asked to describe your strengths, it's good to use words such as "aggressive," "assertive," and "ambitious."

☐ **TRUE**   ☐ **FALSE**

59 If asked, "Tell me about your spouse," the best answer is to advise the interviewer politely that the question is illegal.

☐ **TRUE**   ☐ **FALSE**

60 It's ill advised to ask an applicant, "What branch of the military did you serve in?"

☐ **TRUE**   ☐ **FALSE**

61 "How's your health?" is an illegal question.

☐ **TRUE**   ☐ **FALSE**

62 It's best to show up for an interview at least 20 to 30 minutes early.

☐ **TRUE**   ☐ **FALSE**

63 To prepare for employment interviews, companies always thoroughly read the applicant's resume and sometimes make reference checks before the interview.

☐ **TRUE**   ☐ **FALSE**

64 College honors, self-supported tuition, fraternity or sorority offices held, and the like have little place in the interview.

☐ **TRUE**   ☐ **FALSE**

65 To ease tension and establish rapport with the interviewer in the first five minutes, it's a good idea to tell a joke or two.

☐ **TRUE**   ☐ **FALSE**

66 Smoking or chewing gum during an interview may cause the interviewer to reject an applicant.

☐ **TRUE**   ☐ **FALSE**

67 Common sense dictates that people should dress conservatively for an interview, avoiding gaudy clothing or extreme styles.

☐ **TRUE**   ☐ **FALSE**

68 A winning smile and a firm handshake can make the difference between "winning" or "losing" in an interview.

☐ **TRUE**   ☐ **FALSE**

69 Before the employment interview, the applicant should do some homework on the company. It's poor form to ask the interviewer, "What does your company do?"

☐ **TRUE**   ☐ **FALSE**

70 A supply of resumes, a contact list, a calendar, and a job log are the briefcase contents every job seeker should carry to every interview.

☐ **TRUE**   ☐ **FALSE**

71 What a person says in the interview determines whether he or she gets the offer.

☐ **TRUE**   ☐ **FALSE**

72 When the interviewer says, "Tell me about yourself," the interviewer really wants to know only about your personality.

☐ **TRUE**   ☐ **FALSE**

73 If there are a few applicants for one position, the person with the best technical qualifications generally gets the offer.

☐ **TRUE**   ☐ **FALSE**

74 Most employers are willing to spend time with anyone interested in getting a job in their company.

☐ **TRUE**   ☐ **FALSE**

75 Anytime the national unemployment rate exceeds 9 percent, it's almost impossible to get a job.

☐ **TRUE**   ☐ **FALSE**

76 Pre-employment polygraph (lie-detector) tests are against the law.

☐ **TRUE**   ☐ **FALSE**

77 It's best to look for another job while you are still employed.

☐ **TRUE**   ☐ **FALSE**

78 If a job hunter wants to work in another city, it's best to move there first and then start looking.

☐ **TRUE**   ☐ **FALSE**

79 Most employment managers consider it a breach of ethics for an employee to look for another job on company time.

☐ **TRUE**   ☐ **FALSE**

80 During the interview, it's best to avoid any personal information about family background, marriage, children, or the like.

☐ **TRUE**   ☐ **FALSE**

81 It is illegal for an employer to ask an applicant about marital status or religious background.

☐ **TRUE**   ☐ **FALSE**

82 If a job hunter is divorced, an employer can ask who has custody of the children.

☐ **TRUE**   ☐ **FALSE**

83 Most personnel people regard divorce as a sign of failure, so never volunteer that information in a resume or interview.

☐ **TRUE**   ☐ **FALSE**

84 Always include the statement, "In excellent health," in the personal section of your resume no matter what your health condition is.

☐ **TRUE**   ☐ **FALSE**

85 Beards and long hair on men are still perceived negatively, even if the beard is handsomely trimmed.

☐ TRUE   ☐ FALSE

86 Anyone with graying hair who is looking for a new job had best color or dye it to look younger.

☐ TRUE   ☐ FALSE

87 People over 50, women, blacks, and the unemployed are generally discriminated against in the employment process.

☐ TRUE   ☐ FALSE

88 Most people in the work force are college graduates.

☐ TRUE   ☐ FALSE

89 Reference checks are still an important element of the job search; references should be carefully prepared.

☐ TRUE   ☐ FALSE

90 Employers really don't have the time to verify previous employment or educational background and seldom do so.

☐ TRUE   ☐ FALSE

91 If your references include important people—authors, judges, sports figures—it's a good idea to include them on your resume to make it more impressive.

☐ TRUE   ☐ FALSE

92 Personnel departments cannot legally verify salaries of former employees, so the job hunter can claim any salary he/she likes.

☐ **TRUE**   ☐ **FALSE**

93 Formal employment contracts are usually provided only to senior executives.

☐ **TRUE**   ☐ **FALSE**

94 An employer extending a job offer expects to wait at least three weeks for an answer.

☐ **TRUE**   ☐ **FALSE**

95 A formal offer of employment is a letter outlining title, salary, reporting relationships, benefits, and other important aspects of the job. Without such a letter, there is no formal offer.

☐ **TRUE**   ☐ **FALSE**

96 Temporary work often leads to permanent employment, so it makes sense to accept a temporary job as soon as possible.

☐ **TRUE**   ☐ **FALSE**

97 Getting a good score on a civil service test guarantees a job offer.

☐ **TRUE**   ☐ **FALSE**

98 A company can fire an employee who lied about anything on the employment application form.

☐ **TRUE**   ☐ **FALSE**

99 Sometimes the hiring authority in a department, if sufficiently impressed by the candidate, can create a new job.

☐ **TRUE**   ☐ **FALSE**

100 "Overqualified" is a rejection excuse that really means "too old."

☐ **TRUE**   ☐ **FALSE**

YOUR SCORE

Number of Correct Answers	Comments
Less Than 50	Big Trouble! Don't start your job search until you study the answers and try again.
50-59	At least you got half the answers correct. Of course, you could have done as well flipping a coin. Study the answers and try again.
60-69	Below average, but that's O.K. This book can help you improve your job-hunting skills.
70-79	Average. Who wants to be average? Study the answers to become superb.
80-89	Above average—but you can possibly improve on the next try.

90-95	Excellent—two standard deviations above the mean.
96-99	Superb—you are now ready to succeed in a job search.
100	Impossible. Nobody gets 100!

ABOUT THE AUTHOR

Thomas M. Camden has 30 years' experience as a personnel professional and human resources consultant. He is an officer with EnterChange, Inc., a career transition consulting firm, specializing in corporate change and individual career planning. Previously, he directed his own consulting practice for 15 years. He is a recognized national authority on corporate outplacement and career counseling.

Mr. Camden has served as vice-president of personnel for an investment banking firm and director of personnel for both manufacturing and not-for-profit research and development companies. As a generalist in these positions he has had extensive experience in employment, selection, college relations, policy and procedures development, implementation, employee relations, communications, benefit analysis, and administration.

He is a frequent guest lecturer, TV and radio talk show guest, and author of numerous publications dealing with outplacement, career counseling, and human resources management. His articles appear in professional journals, major national newspapers, and business magazines.

Mr. Camden received a B.S. degree in psychology from Loyola University in Chicago, where he also completed the graduate program in personnel management at the Institute of Human Relations. He is also a graduate of the Executive Program of the University of Chicago Graduate School of Business.

INDEX